COMIC BOOK CHARACTER

UNLEASHING THE HERO IN US ALL

David A. Zimmerman

IVP

InterVarsity Press
Downers Grove, Illino

D0910412

InterVarsity Press
P.O. Box 1400, Downers Grove, IL 60515-1426
World Wide Web: www.ivpress.com
E-mail: mail@ivpress.com

InterVarsity Press® is the book-publishing division of InterVarsity Christian Fellowship/USA®, a student movement active on campus at hundreds of universities, colleges and schools of nursing in the United States of America, and a member movement of the International Fellowship of Evangelical Students. For information about local and regional activities, write Public Relations Dept., InterVarsity Christian Fellowship/USA, 6400 Schroeder Rd., P.O. Box 7895, Madison, WI 53707-7895, or visit the IVCF website at <www.intervarsity.org>.

Scripture quotations, unless otherwise noted, are from the New Revised Standard Version of the Bible, copyright 1989 by the Division of Christian Education of the National Council of the Churches of Christ in the USA. Used by permission. All rights reserved.

Every effort has been made to provide proper credit for material cited in this book. Omissions and errors should be brought to the attention of the publisher for correction in future editions.

Design: Cindy Kiple
Images: Digital Vision

ISBN 0-8308-3260-2
Printed in the United States of America ∞

Library of Congress Cataloging-in-Publication Data

Zimmerman, David, 1970-
  Comic book character: unleashing the hero in us all / David A.
Zimmerman.
    p. cm.
  Includes bibliographical references and index.
  ISBN 0-8308-3260-2 (pbk.: alk paper)
  1. Christian ethics. 2. Comic books, strips, etc.—Religious
aspects—Christianity. I. Title
BJ1251.Z56 2004

                                                                                    2004019200

P	19	18	17	16	15	14	13	12	11	10	9	8	7	6	5	4	3	2	1
Y	19	18	17	16	15	14	13	12	11	10	09	08	07	06	05	04				

To Kara,

super girl and cat woman.

CONTENTS

"We concern ourselves with heroes because they are mirrors in which we see ourselves."

CLARK KENT, A.K.A. SUPERMAN

"A profound thought. . . . He must've read it in a comic book."

PETER PARKER, A.K.A. SPIDER-MAN

INTRODUCTION

We Could Be Heroes

*When people **ask** how to be brave, Supergirl tells them. When people make questions about being brave, Supergirl tells them.*

*Robin wondered what Batman would **expect** from him. He wondered what Batman looked forward to. He was afraid that Batman **expected** too much.*

*Flash would **rather** be good than bad. He would more gladly be good than bad.*

THE SUPER DICTIONARY

Stop me if you've heard this one: A man walks into a phone booth . . .

If the first image to pop into your head is Clark Kent, and if that image is immediately followed by a mental picture of Superman, you're in good company. Superman is a fixture in Western pop culture, so instantly recognizable that people think of a man in tights and a cape instead of the Nietzschean theory that originally gave the term *superman* cultural relevance.

That's a significant comment on contemporary culture: we are more shaped by an entertainment icon than by the major philosopher of the nineteenth century. But Superman, and other superheroes like him, have come to represent what is noble and worth pursuing. Our ethics are reflected in (and perhaps shaped by) who they are; our understanding of salvation and deliverance is shaped by (and perhaps reflected in) their exploits.

Superheroes have cemented their place in the American cultural landscape. A person could wear Spider-Man underwear while riding a Batman rollercoaster, then go home to sit in front of the TV in his Superman (or Wonder Woman) robe watching an *X-Men* DVD, munching on Incredible Hulk cereal. Superheroes have become so culturally viable that even heroes unfamiliar to the mainstream culture such as Daredevil or the Huntress have gotten their own film or television treatments. But where do these heroes come from, and what gives them staying power?

AN ADMITTEDLY SHORT AND SUPERFICIAL HISTORY OF THE UNIVERSAL NEED FOR HEROES

It may seem odd on the surface of things to think that comic books can be linked to Greek myths, but it's not so unusual if you think about it. When I was very young, my parents didn't keep a lot of comic books around the house, but they did have a vast library, and they were interested in having kids who read. Greek myths were easily filtered to a preschooler's reading level and were compelling enough to hold a squirrelly little child's attention.

So I read about Hercules and his twelve adventures, including his battle with the unbeatable Hydra and his encounter with the even more impressive Atlas, who held up the heavens. I read about the Minotaur, the flight of Icarus, the Medusa and the golden fleece. In reading these stories I entered into the storytelling heritage of the Greeks, which taught lessons about the rise and fall of nations and the fragility of the human condition while captivating my imagination with characters of breathtaking power and creativity. My early childhood heroes went way back.

Lest you think I grew up in goatskin pants, raised by pagan parents, I also read stories from the Bible, principally from the Old Testament and the Gospels. I got a kick out of my namesake David, who stood up to a giant and won. Daniel and his friends wowed me as they fought lions and fires and came out unscathed. Even Moses impressed me with his remarkable abilities and his heroic battle against the pharaoh.

By the time I stumbled onto the comic book stand at my local library, I had already been schooled in the classic "hero myths." Not that I believe the Bible is just a bunch of myths, but you have to admit that for a grade-school kid there were some common denominators of interest between Hercules and Samson, Atlas and Goliath. Screenwriter Brian Godawa recognizes the thread that connects the superheroes to these characters from antiquity: "In . . . comic book-based stories there is a projection of super powers onto individuals in much the same way that the gods were projections of pagan hope."

Essentially, every culture in every era has had its mythic heroes—people of extraordinary ability reaching spectacular goals against overwhelming odds. From Abraham's rescue of Lot, to the Maccabees' defense of Jerusalem, to Beowulf's defeat of Grendel, to Saint Patrick's driving out the snakes of Ireland, to Muhammad's siege of Mecca; from William Tell to Robin Hood to Joan of Arc to Catherine the Great to Montezuma to Pancho Villa, people have gravitated to the telling and retelling of stories about people more powerful and more beneficent than they, battling forces more powerful and more malicious than they.

Eventually I turned from religious history and mythology to superheroes and supervillains, and I was quickly an enthusiastic convert. But enough about me, what about *them?*

AN ADMITTEDLY SHORT AND SUPERFICIAL OVERVIEW OF SUPERHEROES

In 1938 the undefined, fledgling comic book industry found its rhythm in

Action Comics #1, where DC Comics introduced a man called Superman. Faster than a speeding bullet, more powerful than a locomotive, able to leap tall buildings in a single bound (of course he couldn't fly; don't be ridiculous), Superman ushered in the era of superheroes. He was followed in short order by others, including *Detective Comics'* Batman, a more sinister and somewhat more plausible hero. Whereas Superman fell to Earth, Batman rose from a family tragedy to fight back against the crime that plagued his city. Whereas Superman had amazing powers, Batman had only his wits, his excellent physique and an immense bank account.

Characters were underdeveloped during this Golden Age of comic books. Print issues were self-contained; kids bought comics to see who needed justice and who needed deliverance, not necessarily to see what their hero was thinking. As the Second World War came to dominate news reports and U.S. families fretted over the fate of their soldiers and their relatives overseas, jingoism overtook comic books. *Captain America Comics* #1, which debuted in 1940 (long before America entered the war), featured a cover picture of Captain America punching Adolf Hitler on the jaw. The character quickly generated sales of millions of books.

After the war some comic book heroes survived and others did not; due to the absence of a running storyline, the fate of particular heroes wasn't terribly important. Instead, as the 1950s unfolded and the industry came under criticism for glamorizing violence and hooliganism among juvenile readers, comic book companies began to focus on brand enhancement. Superman got a superdog, a supercousin and a retrospective on his childhood. Batman got Batwoman and Batgirl. In the process, comics got, well, a little silly.

Until the 1960s, when upstart Marvel Comics launched a flurry of new titles. While flagship DC Comics in 1965 sent Batman prancing around on national TV, Marvel was introducing characters like Spider-Man (1962), a teenage boy exposed to radiation and given enhanced strength and agility; the Incredible Hulk (also 1962), a scientist exposed to radiation and mutated into a raging beast; the Fantastic Four (1961), a group of friends who went into space and gained bizarre powers after being exposed to radia . . . say, are you noticing a pattern? By capitalizing on the uncertainty surrounding nuclear power, Marvel established a new kind of plausibility among comic book superheroes. And to emphasize the blurring of fantasy and reality, Marvel's heroes were placed not in imagined locations like DC's Gotham City or Metropolis but in New York—the capital of the world and the center of the comic book industry.

Perhaps the most significant development in comic books when Marvel entered the scene, however, was that Marvel capitalized on its serial format. Readers started rooting for Peter Parker as he mustered up the courage to ask a girl on a date, even as they booed Spider-Man's enemy, who had a nebulous connection to Parker's daily life. All the while, Parker tried to earn a paycheck by selling photographs of himself as Spider-Man to a newspaper editor who hated Spider-Man's guts. Never mind *Days of Our Lives;* whereas readers could just as easily live without a particular issue of a self-contained comic book, serial comic books were appointment reading. Byron Stump recalls the difference:

> A DC comic, there's a beginning, there's a middle, there's an end. It's complete. . . . A Marvel's going to start in the middle, end in the middle. It'll just be a piece.

The Marvel universe exploded, with wave upon wave of new characters with fascinating origins and complicated life situations. Serialized readers were invested enough in the characters that they wrote in regularly, expanding on character development and providing plausible correctives to errors in the continuity. Marvel editors would indulge such participation by awarding "No Prizes" to people who fixed flawed stories and, as Matthew Pustz observes, "telling the company's readers how smart and hip they were." Comic book readers were becoming a family, and they started to grow up in the 1970s.

Gwen Stacy, the first love of Peter Parker's life and a popular character in the Spider-Man franchise, lost her life in 1973 as a victim by association: Norman Osborne, the mentally unstable father of Peter's best friend, Harry, was the CEO of a laboratory and Spider-Man's arch-nemesis Green Goblin; he discovered that Peter Parker was Spider-Man and used Gwen as bait to draw him out. Gwen died while Peter/Spider-Man and his readers/fans watched helplessly. Comics came closer to real life than ever.

The death of Gwen Stacy was set against a backdrop where Peter Parker's other friends were struggling with other problems plaguing the social conscience of 1970s America. With the support of the U.S. government, Marvel Comics set aside its obligations to the Comics Code Authority in 1971 to show Harry Osborne, another main character in Spider-Man's storyline, struggling with drug use. DC Comics turned heads in 1970-1972 by addressing social justice in its *Green Lantern/ Green Arrow* books; establishment icon Green Lantern was forced by populist anti-hero Green Arrow to face the inequities between rich and poor and systemic racial injustices. Comics in general embraced a mainstream, liberal worldview of tolerance and progressive libertarian ideals.

In 1978 Will Eisner advanced the medium of comic books (or its more sophisticated label "sequential art") with his "graphic novel" *A Contract with God and Other Tenement Stories*. The graphic novel differed from conventional comics in its length, its binding (graphic novels had spines, as opposed to staple-bound comic books, and thus could sit comfortably on a bookshelf) and in many cases its mature and sophisticated content. Comic books now had a template for serious, adult treatment of substantial topics, as well as a format that left behind both serial and situational storytelling. The industry expanded to accommodate Eisner's vision, and by 1989 a Pulitzer Prize had found its way to Art Spiegelman for *Maus: A Survivor's Tale*, a comic book treatment of so grave a subject as the Holocaust.

While the medium of comic books was expanding beyond superheroes, superheroes were expanding into other media: four Superman movies (the first debuting in 1978) and later a series of Batman movies (beginning in 1989); several Spider-Man, Superman and Batman cartoons beginning in the late 1960s; *Wonder Woman* (1976-1979) and *The Incredible Hulk* (1978-1983) television shows in prime time—these and other vehicles increased the mainstream visibility of superhero characters. Though their widespread acceptance didn't necessarily translate into increased comic book sales, they did inaugurate a new era of fascination with fantasy heroes.

This trend crystallized in different ways: satire, in the form of television shows like *The Greatest American Hero* (1981-1983) and later *The Tick* (2001-2002); and more serious treatments such as M. Night Shamalyan's 1998 film *Unbreakable,* which explores how a person comes to himself in discovering his unique gifts, and cult television favorite *Smallville,* a direct revisiting of the Superman origin stories that debuted in 2001 and shows the complexities of growing up different—very different.

> "The proliferation of comic books being adapted into movies signals a contemporary hunger for hero worship, the desire for redemption through the salvific acts of deity."
> BRIAN GODAWA

So comic books and superheroes are entertainment phenomena. But what gives them such potency?

RUNNING ON FAITH FASTER THAN A SPEEDING BULLET

In my own case, comic books rubbed up regularly against core issues of life. My first resource for learning to communicate and for defining the elements that made up my reality was *The Super Dictionary,* a limited-vocabulary resource that used DC Comics characters to give context to the words I was using. I read it cover to cover many times. (Each chapter of this book draws on some of its definitions.) When I was later confirmed in the Catholic church, my aunt gave me a large sum of money in cash, which I put in my pocket as I hopped on my bicycle, rode several miles to my favorite comic book store, and emptied said pockets in exchange for front- and back-issues of *The Avengers, Batman, Daredevil* and *The X-Men.* My scandalized mother made me write my aunt a letter confessing how I had spent her generous gift. I wrote the letter without shame; what else could be worth so much money?

Comic books were, for nonathletic juvenile boys like me, baseball cards and the Mona Lisa and blue-chip stocks all rolled into one. We washed our hands before and after handling them; we carefully inserted them into clear, plastic bags for their protection; we scrupulously read buyers' guides to determine the net worth of our collection; and we stored them in safe places so our unwashed little siblings could not deface them.

Many of those comic books I have lost track of; they're likely circulating through the comic resale underground. But the stories stay in my head, and the connection between those stories and my confirmation remains acute.

I remember the righteous indignation I felt when the X-Men showed me that some people are belittled and discriminated against for no other reason than that they are different. I remember the horror I felt as Captain America listened to a Holocaust survivor recall her time in a Nazi concentration camp. I remember the perplexity that overwhelmed me as Henry Pym, a founding member of the superhero group the Avengers, deteriorated from heroic genius to broken down emotional wreck, betraying his teammates and beating his wife mercilessly. How could such a hero fall so far? And if my hero could fall, what might happen to me?

Somewhere along the way comic book characters moved from being two-dimensional—good guys and bad guys fighting in brightly colored tights—to being human. And while that conversion was unsettling to my adolescent mind, my adult mind reflects on it every once in a while. I take lessons from them now that were only vague considerations then. You might say that I followed a comic book catechism.

A COMIC BOOK CATECHISM

In this book I hope to give some order to that catechism, to mine the characters who have led the genre for what they suggest about what is true and right in the world, and what happens when the values they put before us rub up against the values embraced in American culture and the Christian tradition. While I won't be laying out a systematic program for becoming super—as though each of us is only a series of steps from a perfect life—I will be painting a portrait of how each of us, regardless of our peculiar abilities or flaws or circumstances, grows into our understanding and practice of virtue. I'll be looking at a number of issues that comic book heroes address in explicit and subtle ways, and drawing lines from them to the reality we face.

Why are we sometimes so strong and yet often so weak? What makes the difference between righteous anger and blind rage? Why do superheroes (and we) wear masks? What's so super about being good looking, young or even simply alive? Why are we so quick to marginalize people? Which higher power ought we to submit ourselves to, and which ought we to rebel against—the government? our peers and ourselves? our Creator? Who will save us from this body of death? And how then shall we live?

These are core questions we each must face in the world we inhabit. They've been answered in comic books, and they're being answered in our lived experience. Sometimes those answers correspond, and sometimes they don't. But as testing a car in extreme weather conditions flushes out its strengths and limitations, so by testing what appears to

be virtuous or axiomatic in the extreme caricatures of comic book superheroes, we can discover what is truly true, good, right and noble.
And once we've fixed our mind on these things, we can get on with living a heroic life.

LET THE WEAK SAY "I AM STRONG"

Spider-Man, Superman & the Incredible Hulk

*Batgirl's **body** is strong. All the parts of her are strong. She says that good food makes strong **bodies.***

***Everyone** would like to be as strong as Wonder Woman. All people would like to be that strong.*

THE SUPER DICTIONARY

Hear the phrase "comic book reader," and many people immediately picture a gangly, pimply loser. Outside of prepubescent boys, the majority demographic audience for comic books is, let's face it, postpubescent boys. And the older we get, the more fiercely committed we must become to the fantasy universe mapped out in sequential art in order to keep the title "fanboy." Sadly, however, the more fiercely committed we become to comic book fantasy, the less comfortable we feel in the reality we actually inhabit. The comic book (and later the film) *American Splendor* touches on this sense of surreality for those of us who filter our lives through comic books—we become to our own minds caricatures of ourselves, and our engagement of the world is paneled off into isolated en-counters. Author Richard Reynolds highlights the dilemma: "The comic book . . . continues to be . . . held by many to be an irredeemably corrupt and corrupting form of discourse, or else suitable only for chil-dren and the semi-literate." Fanboys in particular are forced to deny our fasci-nation with superheroes, to accept as true our classification by the general public as geeky weirdos, or to live in the uncomfortable tension some-where in between: *He seems so nor-mal otherwise . . .*

"Comic book stories presented physical strength and appearance as the measure of an individual's worth, while the ads offered children the supposed means for achieving it."

BRADFORD W. WRIGHT

You've surely come across a pic-ture of the stereotypical fanboy. The TV show *The Simpsons* has a recurring example: an overweight, smug pseudo-intellectual resembling not at all the heroes he promotes. He celebrates superhuman strength, but in his real, everyday life he is weak, contributing nothing positive to his community.

That's OK, though, because comic books cater to the weak. When I was very young, growing up in Iowa, I responded to an ad in a comic book promising me muscles that would ripple every time I combed my hair or drank a bottle of soda, a physique that would make my arch-enemies think twice before kicking sand in my face when I went to the Iowa beaches. I was weak, but for the cost of postage (plus, say, $6 ship-ping and handling) I could be strong.

When the package arrived I ripped it open to find a sixteen-page booklet. Fifteen pages had pictures of a ridiculously burly guy doing ba-sic exercises in a variety of household settings—situps using the sofa as a brace for his legs, pushups from the seat of a chair, that sort of thing. The sixteenth page invited me to send away for more materials that would turn me into a hulking behemoth and keep my face free of all that Iowa sand I was apparently so afraid of. I did a few situps before realizing I had been hoodwinked out of my money. So I went back and read the comic book.

THE SECRET LIFE OF THE SUPERPOWERED

Fortunately for my fragile psyche, the comic book offered more than cheap marketing tactics to fulfill my fantasies of strength and self-defense. In fact, superheroes often serve as stand-ins for the shut-outs among their audience. Though our heroes live out their daily lives meek and mild-mannered, their nights are filled with heroic action and stunning feats.

Consider a typical day for a junior-high-aged hero. In the tradition of matching initials (from Lois Lane to Bruce Banner), let's call him Fritz Fryling. Fritz wakes up, tucks his wings into an oversized shirt and walks to school—even though he could fly. As he reaches his gym locker, he hears behind him the first of many taunts from the class bully: "There's Owl-boy. I hope you don't lose those Coke-bottle glasses of yours during dodge ball. Hoot hoot!" Then our mutant friend feels the sharp sting of a wet towel snapped against his legs.

He knows he could spin his head all the way around to face his attacker; he knows that he could easily fly out of reach of the towel; he even knows that his razor-sharp, retractable talons could quickly shred a bully whom no one would miss for long. He knows that he's smarter and nicer to girls than the bully; he even knows that in reality he's stronger and more dangerous than the bully. But he stays silent, and he keeps his secret.

That's just gym class. We, the readers, know what our hero's classmates, teachers and family don't know, and we sympathize with his plight. And in a way, we share in his suffering because we are all too familiar with the pain of alienation, of victimization. We know that bullies call the shots in junior high and that one moment of satisfaction in returning violence against a popular, powerful nemesis would open the door to all kinds of trouble.

We know this whether we are the bullied or the bully. There are social forces at work in our lives, whatever season we find ourselves in. We are part of a pecking order because fallen human beings operate consciously and unconsciously in power dynamics. When we are weak, we wish we were strong. When we are strong, we fight to retain our strength.

I'd like to pretend, for example, that I was always the victim of such bullying and never the perpetrator, but I can't. I certainly could have been: when I was a child, I was hardly ever in the in-crowd. I was a band geek who collected comic books, for heaven's sake. As such, I was manipulated into helping pretty girls cheat on their finals, I was called a nerd and a loser to my face, and I was pointed out for public ridicule and threatened with a beating on more than one occasion.

> "Superheroes are first and foremost about role-playing—becoming the character."
>
> SCOTT McCLOUD

And yet, I managed to find a way of asserting myself within the caste I found myself in. My friends and I invented ways of ostracizing people that would cause maximum pain—the most unimaginative being "the group" membership cards we passed out to those people we considered part of our A-list. (Imagine the humiliation of being rejected for membership in a group of nerds.) At my worst, I made a girl cry all the way home from school, and I beat up a boy for being too new to our town. I didn't have much social power to defend, but I defended what little I did have with ferocity.

But back to our hero. Fritz trudges his way through a day filled with occasional humiliations and the constant awareness that at any moment he could overturn the power dynamics in place. That night he hits the streets, with wings spread wide open and talons extended. He is no longer Owl-boy; now he is Night Vision, ready to use his power without restraint against whatever forces of evil threaten the peace.

And so are we. Just as our hero has escaped his everyday world to live free as his expanded self, so his readers leave behind the frustrations of paying bills and finishing homework and avoiding trouble and enduring rejection to play hero.

THE FANTASY OF STRENGTH

So what is it about superheroes that makes them endure the tedium of normal life? And why do we, as readers, allow it? If we had the powers of our heroes, would we stand for the petty meanness of the average people who bully us? If we knew our friends had such powers, would we allow them to do nothing for us or for themselves? There's an unspoken rule among superheroes that powers are to be used only in critical situations. We're not often told why, but the origin of one superhero gives us a look at what could happen without such self-restraint.

Spider-Man wasn't always Spider-Man. For most of his childhood he was mild-mannered Peter Parker, an orphaned genius being raised by his elderly aunt and uncle. He was a bookish, withdrawn kid, regularly used and abused by his classmates. He was Owl-boy without the wings.

Then one day on a field trip to a laboratory, Peter was bitten by a spider exposed to radiation. Over time Peter discovered that he had appropriated the physical characteristics of a spider—the ability to stick to walls and ceilings; greatly enhanced strength, speed and agility; and (we're told much later in the 2002 film) the capacity to spin his own webbing. He had always been smarter than anyone in his class; now he was stronger, faster, more talented and quickly more confident as well.

So Peter did what you might expect the butt of everyone's jokes to do: he started showing off. He picked fights with schoolmates and got quick revenge on the people who had abused him for so long, and he started making lots of money by exploiting his newfound talents as an unbeatable mystery wrestler. He alienated everyone he encountered—his employer, his classmates, eventually even the press—with his brash, defiant attitude. And when he could have stopped a burglary without even exerting himself, he didn't bother. All the average, immature high-school students got their comeuppance from Peter, but no bad guys met justice through Spider-Man.

Peter learned a painful lesson though. His uncle, who had raised him since his parents' death, lost his life at the hands of the very burglar Peter had let escape. Peter quickly realized that by his inaction he was complicit in his uncle's death. And by the end of his first adventure, as he meditated on his uncle's advice—"With great power comes great responsibility"—he grew up a bit and discovered the proper channel for his abilities.

Peter Parker added an adolescent humanness to superheroes that until his debut in the comic *Amazing Fantasy* had played a minor role, and he resonated with his readers. We learned that to fantasize about having special powers was all well and good, but there was a corresponding ethic to having such powers, and our fantasies would not play out as we might like if we intended to remain the hero of our own stories. We can hope that someday we will be stronger than we are, better equipped to handle the hardships we inevitably face, but we must also hope that we will use that strength with wisdom and humility.

For Peter, that humility meant returning day after day to school and eventually to work, enduring humiliation as well as he could, and seeking the appropriate balance of power and responsibility that his uncle had pointed him toward. He used his powers only against those whose passions could not be controlled by the ordinary safeguards of law, common decency and moral impulse. He alternately used and hid his powers so that he and the people around him could live as normal and happy a life as possible. Such was his gift, and such was the greatest use of his strength.

WILLING WEAKNESS

Unlike Peter Parker, Superman was born Superman. He was christened Kal-El on another world but raised on Earth as mild-mannered Clark

Kent, a lovable nerd in a world too big for him. But why would someone who could do anything and be anyone choose to remain Clark Kent? Is there something inherently virtuous in being weak? Does Superman practice deceit as a part of everyday life?

You could blame his adoptive parents. They hid his unearthly origin from their friends and neighbors, and brought up Superman from infancy as their own. They advised him to keep his abilities secret, and when he left home he continued to do so. They raised him to live a dual life.

To be asked by those in authority over you to not be who you are seems patently unfair, but the whole thing seems particularly absurd in the case of Superman. His parents couldn't stop him from being Superman unless he let them. He condescended from birth to adopt the lifestyle handed him by his parents.

Superman embraced his identity as Clark Kent. In fact, Clark Kent's weakness became as much an asset to Superman as heat vision or the power of flight—it kept for him some sense of normalcy that would otherwise be unachievable, given his particular gifts. It also meant that people regularly underestimated him, allowing him to work some angles of a problem with significantly less resistance than he would have experienced in cape and costume.

Superman does, however, have more than one weakness of his own. He can be affected by the supernatural, for example, which means that he can be coerced into situations beyond his capacity to escape or overpower. But supernatural events are by their definition outside of what is normal to our experience. Over the course of a normal day there are only a couple of weaknesses that stick with him.

EYE HAS NOT SEEN

The first of Superman's weaknesses is not so much a weakness as it is a limitation: though he can see through virtually anything, he cannot see through lead. You and I survive our daily lives happily enough without

X-ray vision, but then again, we don't have to see through anything to get our work done—unless you count seeing through scheming and posturing by the people in our lives.

But Superman lives his life in part by seeing through things. In hostage situations he can know where all the criminals and victims are hidden—unless they are shielded with lead. As a reporter Clark Kent can investigate a suspicious corporation without ever making it past the reception desk—as long as the building is not lined with lead. He can see things he's not supposed to see (like birthday presents) and know things he's not supposed to know (like the contents of a safety deposit box) as long as no lead blocks his view.

Now let's be frank: this isn't much of a weakness or limitation. Superman can do virtually anything else, so he can easily find his way around the lead issue; he can even rip the lead apart if he's desperate enough to get it out of his way. A more interesting weakness would be if he couldn't see through air or glass.

But Superman has occasionally suffered for his inability to see through lead, most notably in the first *Superman* motion picture, in which his rival Lex Luthor uses a lead-lined box to hide the more dangerous of Superman's weaknesses.

THE THING TO AVOID

Superman's other weakness is also not so much a weakness as it is a vulnerability: though he is impervious to virtually all earthly elements in any form or combination, his physical or mental state is compromised whenever he comes into contact with kryptonite, the piecemeal remains of the planet of his birth.

Kryptonite comes in forms conveniently distinguished by color. When exposed to green kryptonite, for example, Superman is quickly sapped of his powers, his strength and ultimately his life force. Too much green kryptonite for too long, and Superman dies.

Red kryptonite isn't necessarily fatal; its effects are entirely unpredictable. Red kryptonite has been known to change Superman's shape or his constitution; sometimes it simply renders him powerless. Sometimes, though, as happened in an early episode of the TV show *Smallville,* he becomes violent, self-absorbed, immoral—all the things you would not want an unstoppable force to be. Under the influence of red kryptonite Superman has hurt people he cares about, caused rampant destruction to places important to him and generally undone much of the good he'd done previously. Too much red kryptonite for too long, and the soul of Superman dies.

Fortunately for him and for those who inhabit his universe, Superman recognizes and accepts his limitations and vulnerabilities. He can't see through lead—so what? That doesn't make him less of a person. He has to depend on other people when he gets sick from exposure to green kryptonite—so what? We all need other people from time to time. He can't let himself fall under the influence of red kryptonite—so what? We all have issues that overwhelm our sensibilities, and if we're lucky we find the strength and support to steer clear of their influence.

Superman is lucky. He knows and accepts what he can and cannot do, and he accepts the help of people in his times of need. His weaknesses, though they are profound, do not define him and will not overcome him. The Hulk, on the other hand, frequently wallows in his weakness and gives uncontrolled expression to the rage his weaknesses incite.

HIDEOUS STRENGTH

Unlike any of his predecessors in the comic book universe, the Hulk explores the pitfalls of strength. He came to be as the result of a heroic act by a physically weak and ethically challenged scientist who was developing a weapon of mass destruction for the U.S. government. To save the life of a young drifter, Bruce Banner enters the weapons testing range and is exposed to gamma radiation. Now, since Bruce isn't killed by the

bomb, we might simply conclude that it is a failure and he is a bad scientist. But the effect of the radiation on Bruce keeps us reading.

We soon discover that Bruce, when faced with stressful circumstances, morphs into a primal, raging beast who gives near-full vent to his emotions. So what do the people around him start doing? You guessed it—they consistently expose Bruce to stressful circumstances.

> *"The Hulk is the manifestation of the part of yourself that you're trying to deny. · · · He's the big unknown that is hiding in the deepest level of brain structure."*
>
> ANG LEE

Creator Stan Lee characterizes the Hulk as a sort of Jekyll-Hyde character, but unlike Mr. Hyde, the Hulk is always sympathetic—always the protagonist. Predating revolutionary movements of the 1960s such as the Black Panthers and the Weathermen, the Hulk served as guilty pleasure, occasionally sticking it to the government that persecuted him and generally wallowing in righteous self-pity.

As a rampaging, paranoid beast, the Hulk doesn't fit the description "team player," but he has been attached to teams nonetheless. The Avengers and, later, the Defenders had to step lightly around the Hulk and channel his rage toward their own goals, but for a short time the Hulk experienced the security and insecurities that coexist in a team setting.

Still, for the most part the Hulk has been a loner. In a universe given to exaggeration, the Hulk serves as an exaggerated example of the isolation that accompanies power and difference. In this respect he is different only in degree from our Fritz Fryling/Night Vision, from Peter Parker, from Superman, even from each of us.

The Hulk is the favorite character of Brian, a friend of mine. Brian runs a successful business that as a side effect leaves him without direct human contact for hours at a time. Unmarried, he's watched friends and family members get married and have children—something he wishes for himself. He works, eats and sleeps alone while others work, eat and sleep together. Sometimes it drives him, well, a little crazy.

Yet Brian has an enviable life when judged on its own merits. He controls the direction of his business; he enjoys a reputation as a gifted, ethical businessperson and as a generous, compassionate person; he has a diverse network of friends who are intensely (and, I admit, intrusively) devoted to his best interests. He is, at least in theory, free to go anywhere and do anything at virtually any time. Brian and the Hulk have this in common: they are, depending on your mood, free or cursed to roam the earth.

STRENGTH IN WEAKNESS

Superman has something, then, that the Hulk does not. Superman has accepted what he is *not* as part of embracing what he *is*. Granted, it's good to be Superman; he isn't hunted like the Hulk or misunderstood like Spider-Man. He does recognize, however, that his weaknesses play their part in shaping who he is and what he does. Matters that require seeing through lead and handling kryptonite will have to be delegated to someone else, but outside of those examples virtually anything looks like a job for Superman.

We're all in many ways like these heroes. Despite our best efforts some people will be intimidated enough by our strengths that they will try to manipulate our weaknesses. We live in a politicized world, and even the best of us are motivated enough by personal gain to be threatened or opportunistic in how we relate to others. I've been jealous of my friends' successes, and I've manipulated the mistakes made by professional colleagues to my own advantage, and—trust me—I'm not alone. We've all been on either side of Spider-Man's webbing.

Like the Hulk, we will continually face the temptation of interpreting our differences as weaknesses and wallowing in what we cannot be or do, even lashing out at convenient scapegoats. The American propensity to sue corporations for emotional damage over such things as making their food too fatty is a good example of pent-up frustration expressing itself blindly. Each of us is one gamma-ray bomb away from being the Hulk.

But like Superman, when we come to terms with our limits and embrace our identity we are freed to experience the surprising strength that can flow through our weakness. The apostle Paul understood this for himself and for his hearers. "Not many of you were wise," he writes matter-of-factly in 1 Corinthians 1:26. Yet the Corinthians lack of wisdom made it all the more remarkable that, as Paul goes on to suggest, they held the secrets to life and joy and peace. In fact, their foolishness—our foolishness—would "shame the wise" and bring glory to God. "Therefore," he would later declare, "I will *boast* all the more gladly of my *weaknesses,* . . . for whenever I am weak, then I am strong" (2 Corinthians 12:9-10, emphasis added).

Many have wished that they were like Spider-Man or Superman or the Hulk or even the apostle Paul. But few have wished to be like them in their weakness. Perhaps that's why so few have been so strong.

VENGEANCE IS MINE

Batman, the Joker & the Punisher

*Batman is **busy** fighting a bad man. He is at work fighting. Batman is **busier** when another man begins to fight. And he is **busiest** when everyone starts to fight.*

*Green Lantern can be a fierce **warrior.** He can be a fierce fighter. He has fought some terrible **warriors.***

THE SUPER DICTIONARY

So, superheroes are typically strong, and their alter egos are often weak. There must be a bridge, something that weaves one into the other. In most cases, that has something to do with tragedy.

Some traumatic event is inherent to a good deal of origin stories. Consider Bruce Wayne, the child of wealthy parents in a healthy community. One night as he and his folks happily head home after a night at the movies, they are stopped on the street by a burglar. Bruce's parents are shot dead, and though Batman will not prowl the streets of Gotham City for some twenty years yet, he is born that night.

There are exceptions, of course. Superman has no violent trauma to plague his psyche—unless you count the utter annihilation of his home planet. The Fantastic Four have no anguish to their origin story, except perhaps for the trauma Ben Grimm experienced as the radiation he was exposed to transformed him into what could only be called "the Thing." These examples are mild compared to the bitterness of losing parents, children, eyesight or, for characters such as Spawn, the Crow or Deadman, life itself.

Superpowered beings are typically physically strong and often emotionally wounded. How they use their strength and channel their pain helps us to decide if they are heroes, villains or something in between.

THE GOOD

Bruce Wayne had everything you might want growing up. He was the only child of insanely wealthy parents, he lived on the expansive grounds of a stately manor, he had a guaranteed future as the head of his father's corporate empire, and he was secure in the fact that he was loved— based not only on the love and affection he received from his parents but also on, of all things, the lifelong committed service of a butler named Alfred.

"What makes Batman so different . . . is that his character is formed by confronting a world which refuses to make sense."

RICHARD REYNOLDS

None of that was taken from him upon the death of his parents. He still had a secure base and an enviable future, but immediately he applied himself to avenging their death.

Bruce practiced various forms of hand-to-hand combat, studied forensic science and learned enough mechanical engineering to help him develop tools and weapons for his planned vengeance. He spent the remainder of his adolescence not only training to fight back against the city that had orphaned him but establishing a decoy identity, a persona devoted to self-indulgent hedonism for whom the death of his parents held no lasting hurt. And when he and his alter ego were ready, he returned home to set up shop. A compelling account of his first year as a vigilante is given in Frank Miller's *Batman: Year One.*

"[A superhero's] methods may be those of a bully . . . [but] his alleged motives make him a hero."

FRANK VLAMOS

Bruce Wayne is eager to step into the crime scene in Gotham City, but for all his training he isn't prepared to face the full threat of a city plagued with petty and organized crime, a corrupt justice system and an ambivalent public. He quickly discovers that, as a force for change, he will act largely on his own. In a sense this leaves him at a great advantage, since he can act at his own pace, as covertly as possible and according to his own conscience. But it also means he has some decisions to make.

One decision is to define his limits. "I'm no killer!" he reminds himself as, on his first night out in costume, three teenage petty thieves panic at the sight of him and one almost falls to his death from a fire escape. And yet, why isn't Batman a killer? He's immersed himself in the art of combat since he witnessed the violent death of the most important people in his life. Batman is undeniably violent, committing "seventy-eight acts of assault in [his first] five weeks." But he stops short of killing people. Killing is bad, but hurting is acceptable. Batman has drawn his first line.

An intrigued police lieutenant, James Gordon (who will become a staple in Batman's life), launches a sting operation to flush Batman out, but it takes a random accident for Gordon to catch sight of him. Batman is wise to the police's efforts, so he stays hidden until he sees a bag lady in the path of an out-of-control car. To intervene will expose him to the police. He makes his second ethical decision: the safety of innocent people is more important than his own security. He also makes a positive move: he not only fights crime, he protects the innocent. Suddenly the vigilante cannot be so narrowly defined.

As the police close in on him, he fights his way free, but not before saving a cat from being shot (and ferociously punishing the person who tried to shoot it) and leaving money at an abandoned men's clothing store in exchange for a quick disguise. Third ethical decision: innocents will not suffer for his vendetta.

Batman is at war, no question, and he wastes no time fantasizing that his war will be brought to a quick conclusion. But Batman's war is tempered by his positive agenda: beyond punishing the guilty, Batman decides to seek the redemption of his city. That's what makes him and others like him—from good cop Jim Gordon to future sidekick Robin—heroes.

But Bruce Wayne is not the only person in Gotham City to suffer trauma. The person who would become his nemesis had his origin in tragedy, and the way he dealt with his tragedy guaranteed violence and chaos for the rest of his life.

THE BAD

The Joker is as evil as need be. At times his storytellers characterize him as disturbingly vile; at other times he is made a parody of himself. He can be as vicious and heartless as the audience can bear, as cruel or benign as the storyline commands.

In his first appearance in *Batman* #1 (1941), the Joker was the latest in a series of imaginative villains for Batman to defeat, but his character—from his choice of costume, to his name, to his method—had a great deal of potential for storytelling, and he became a staple for Batman stories by the 1950s. Widespread social concern over comic books' effects on juvenile delinquency, however, led to the creation of a severely restrictive code of content so the nature of the business in that era became to tame the villains and the heroes, till crime resembled elaborate pranks and fighting evil was akin to fighting rivals on the playground.

Still, the Joker was the go-to villain for epic stories. He was eventually responsible for the death (in 1988) of Robin and (also in 1988) the crippling of Batgirl. The first *Batman* movie makes the Joker responsible for the death of Bruce Wayne's parents; it also makes Batman responsible for the Joker's origin, making the polarities of Batman and the Joker a complex interweaving of good and evil. What continually brings the two characters together are their competing goals for Gotham City: where Batman hopes to impose peace, security and order on a city in crisis, the Joker seeks to release what he sees as the city's inherent chaos and meaninglessness.

To actualize his vision, the Joker had to make his own set of decisions, summed up in the presumption that his own agenda supersedes the agendas of others. Such a conclusion allows him to victimize others for his own gain. He manipulates institutions of civil order, from the police to the United Nations to network television, toward his own ends. He destroys people randomly, for his own amusement, to express his consternation or "to prove a point," as he elaborates in Alan Moore's *Batman: The Killing Joke*.

> Madness is the emergency exit. . . . You can just step outside, and close the door on all those dreadful things that happened. You can lock them away . . . forever.

The Joker's origin proposed by Moore is similar to Batman's except for the victim's interpretation. Bruce Wayne is given a cause that effects his parents' death. Problem: crime and apathy plague a world that could otherwise be wonderful. Solution: fight crime, combat apathy. But what happens to a man whose world is not so wonderful when the only person in the world who sees value in him, his pregnant wife, is electrocuted by a baby-bottle heater? when ambivalent colleagues manipulate his emotions toward their own end? when a vat of chemicals burns his skin and destroys any hope for a normal life?

Other origin accounts tell the Joker's story differently. The movie *Batman,* for example, paints the picture of a lifelong criminal whose methods—though not his motivations—are transformed when toxic chemicals destroy his body. In the film, the Joker dies in a random act of serendipitous justice but is resurrected as a version of himself filtered into pure evil. But beyond the villain's origin is the villain's agenda, which never really changes: to gain the world no matter the cost and to recenter it on himself. In Moore's story, the Joker attempts to redefine reality for his captive audience:

> The average man! Physically unremarkable, it has instead a deformed set of values. Notice the hideously bloated sense of humanity's importance. The club-footed social conscience and the withered optimism. . . .
>
> Most repulsive of all, are its frail and useless notions of order and sanity. If too much weight is placed upon them . . . they snap.
>
> How does it live, I hear you ask? How does this poor, pathetic specimen survive in today's harsh and irrational world? The sad answer is "not very well." Faced with the inescapable fact that human existence is mad, random and pointless, one in eight of them crack and go stark slavering buggo! Who can blame them? In a world as psychotic as this . . . any other response would be crazy!

See the logic? To not be crazy is to be crazy. The Joker sees himself as a messiah of sorts—"Be mad, as I am mad"—but he competes for the title against others, from Superman's nemesis Lex Luthor to the X-Men's enemy Magneto (both of whom will be discussed in chapter ten). Seeking control by any means necessary and promoting yourself no matter the cost to others: these are what make the Joker, and others like him, villains.

THE COMPLICATED

Somewhere in between can be found vigilantes who don't ascend to the level of hero. In fact, to call them heroes would be to make a defiant statement, in a similar way that calling members of antigovernment militias "heroes" makes a statement. Their actions are motivated by a clearly defined view of the world around them, but their behavior defies culturally accepted standards of fair play. To call such people heroes is to imply that anyone who condemns their actions is either sympathetic to or in league with the cause of society's ills.

If heroes, measured against the standard of Batman, are responsible contributors to society—they seek the good of their city—these "antiheroes" are reactors, often in the nuclear sense. Like Batman or the Joker, they experience some sort of traumatic event. Like Batman, they see a clear cause for their trauma. Like the Joker, all bets are off when it comes to confronting that cause.

The murder of Frank Castle's wife and kids prompted him to become the Punisher. Falling back on his military combat training and funding his efforts from a small family fortune, he drops out of society to make his battle against crime a full-time occupation. His costume is simple: a skull on a black shirt, a leather jacket and a lot of military weaponry. He doesn't bother to hide his face, in part because he has no secret alter ego to protect, in part because he doesn't intend to leave behind survivors who could identify him.

The Punisher's methods set him at odds against people who would otherwise be sympathetic to his cause. Heroes such as Spider-Man and Daredevil occasionally enter into a guarded, temporary alliance with him when they have a common enemy, but such collaboration ends as soon as they catch the bad guys and have to decide what to do with them. Heroes want to turn them over to the police; the Punisher wants to shoot them in the head.

Because the Punisher is always at war, he thinks strategically in every situation, which often leads him to make temporary concessions to the crime syndicate he's sworn to fight. He makes use of petty criminals as informants for as long as they serve his purposes; in the first issue of *Punisher: War Zone,* one such informant no longer serves such a purpose, so the Punisher kills him. In the *Daredevil* storyline, we find the Punisher serving a prison sentence amid scores of criminals he helped to put away. He tells one of them, an assassin called Bullseye, of an opportunity to escape. Bullseye accepts the advice but asks why the Punisher would help him out: "You're likely to do something stupid and get yourself killed. I'd like that."

The Punisher is not the only person to have been traumatized by violent crime, and for those who ache for revenge the Punisher is a hero who has earned their trust and support. But the Punisher is unique in his total commitment. His sympathizers typically don't withdraw from society, and at a certain point as they process their grief, they have to decide whether to surrender fully to the pursuit of vengeance or to seek a normal life. Eventually, the Punisher knows, his allies will part ways, and he will be left alone.

"The negotiation of a character's heroism (or villainy) is fleshed out, as in all narrative, by the examination of moral choices made under pressure."

RICHARD REYNOLDS

The Punisher is not quite bad, not quite good. His agenda is too narrow to be either and too all-consuming to be easily classified. For all the Punisher's strategizing, he is fundamentally a victim lashing out in blind rage; for all his pontificating about justice, he has neither the time nor the inclination to offer a positive agenda to a crime-ridden community. We may pity him, we may understand him, we are even expected to cheer him on in the tales of his exploits, but if we are to be whole persons in a healthy community, we cannot call him hero.

THE ETHICS OF PAIN

Nevertheless, the Punisher is there, as are villains such as the Joker and heroes such as Batman. Each offers a vision for facing the senseless trauma that occasionally invades our lives. Our visceral reaction is to lash out: to seek revenge against the people or systems that led to our pain, to curse God for allowing our suffering. Beyond lashing out, we are tempted to dwell on our trauma, even to wallow in our feelings of anguish: our relation to other people and a life that transcends such localized trauma demands that, before we can move on, we must make sense of it.

Certainly we can be sympathetic to people who have suffered acute trauma such as physical or sexual abuse. Their suffering can be given no defense. But beyond the experience of suffering is the challenge to live on, which demands of the sufferer a decision of the will to move beyond the trauma and re-engage life as it unfolds. That decision is an ethical one, for how we live in the aftermath of trauma has implications for people beyond the victim. It would be a crime, no matter how sympathetic the jury, for a victim of rape to hunt down and kill the rapist—because it is a crime to kill. It would be tragic, no matter how understanding the partner, for a victim of rape to permanently withdraw emotionally from her spouse, or for a victim of child abuse to tolerate as an adult the abuse of his own children. It would be a pity for a person who tries but fails to find a satisfactory meaning for her suffering to conclude that her life is therefore meaningless.

We can sin in the wake of traumatic events by using them as proof that nothing in life works and by indulging our indignation by any means necessary. But that is the way of the vigilante, the way of the villain. To acknowledge that vengeance is not ours to seek and to instead seek the good more earnestly—that is the way of the hero.

X-CURSUS

Heroes in the
Hands of a Professional

*Flash was on **television.** He was on the set that shows pictures and sounds of things happening far away. Many people saw him on their **televisions.***

*Lois Lane needed to **complete** the story she was writing. She needed to finish it. After she **completed** her work, she could go out to lunch.*

THE SUPER DICTIONARY

You're called into a meeting, and at the meeting you're invited by one of the biggest media conglomerates in the world to write stories about one of their principal franchises. And you have no idea who they're talking about.

If this were to happen to you, your name might be Todd Komarnicki, a rising star in film and television. He was in the midst of producing the 2003 hit holiday movie *Elf* when he was approached by Warner Brothers Television to write, executive-produce and run a show about the Flash. He had already had two novels published and directed one film—*Resistance,* a love story set in World War II. He had also previously sold six pilots for television production—no mean feat in a field overrun with writers clamoring for a breakthrough. But the Flash would be the first one to be filmed. "So much about Hollywood is perseverance only. Until *Elf* I've been making a living and building a life and having a company really based on my reputation among about fifty people on the planet."

Success in television is measured in incremental steps: sell a script, shoot the pilot, edit the pilot, present it to network executives, and if all goes well, watch your scripts come to life on TV. And that's not even the last step. "If the network likes the pilot they usually commit to about thirteen episodes. Those shows air on television, and more scripts are contracted based on ratings."

So Todd had his work cut out for him, both because of the complexities of successfully negotiating a television show and because he had no background with a superhero who'd had three distinct alter egos over a fifty-year history.

"I didn't know the story of the Flash. I was a complete neophyte. I called my producing partner on the way home, and he freaked out. 'That is my favorite character of all time!' He sent me all these old comics in mylar comic bags. Paul Levitz and Gregory Noveck from DC helped me to soak up the material. It was important for me to get to know the Flash so that I could tell an authentic story. I know what it's like to create something from nothing, and I know what the Flash means to people. So I approached this task with great humility, great respect."

On the surface, of course, there's not much to know about the Flash. "Lots of superheroes have super-speed *plus* some other power. The Flash has got super-speed, and that's all. Turning that into something deeper and, for me, more emotionally and spiritually relevant became the task."

The Flash ultimately became a story about being human and wrestling with extraordinary circumstances, which fits well into the way other comic books have translated to live-action television.

"The studio wanted to tap into the success of *Smallville* by following that show's 'no tights, no flights' formula. We see Clark Kent—not Superman—living as regular a life as possible. On *The Flash,* you won't see the red costume or the lightning logo. You'll see a guy who's been drifting, kind of selfish. Once he discovers that he has super-speed, all that changes. He determines that the rest of his life will be in service to others. To me it's a show about finding who you're supposed to be—your identity—and living it out boldly, playing your part in the world."

Costumes are an incredibly important aspect of comic book storytelling, but they tend to get in the way on screen. Besides, there are other ways of addressing the theme of secrets and benevolent deception. " 'No tights, no flights' places all the hero's secrets *within* the human being. Other people can't experience what they experience; they can only see the results of it. The outfit is really almost secondary. It's almost like his disguise is his own human flesh.

"Imagine saving people and being on the cover of magazines and stuff. . . . That's what I was thinking. Smash evil and be popular. I had no idea I'd be doing laundry and listening to people whine all the time. These are the battles TV never tells you about."

SPEEDY, FASTEST SIDEKICK ALIVE

"When you move from one medium to another, you have to adapt. If you try to mimeograph the comic, you have to wonder why you bother. It's the difference between doing karaoke and doing a fresh interpretation of the song. At the same time, the core values in *The Flash* TV show—acting quickly, putting others first, living a heroic, sacrificial life—are endemic in the original."

Todd is on a writing retreat as we talk, so the script is fresh in his mind. He sets his series in gritty, modern-day New York City. "The comic is set in an imaginary town, but I felt that took us out of it, made it too dreamy. J. B. Finn is the new Flash, but we find out that his father, Wally West from the comic, was the Flash before him. Max Mercury (from the comic) is a mentor to J. B.; Linda Park and Tina McGee are future love interests; and police detective Henry Paulsen will serve as a sort of adviser. J. B.'s best friend is a totally new character, Pedro Martinez, who knows his secret. That's the fundamental relationship. Pedro represents the audience in the show. He's known J. B. since before he was the Flash, and now he can't believe he gets to be so close to greatness.

"Every week J. B. receives a DVD that shows a crime taking place in the future. J. B. has to figure out where and when the crime takes place, and then he has to run fast enough that he winds up in the future to stop the crime. While he's away, he's missing his own life in the present. The cost of his efforts is that he misses who he is—his youth, his life. His motto is 'Live fast so others don't die young.' "

Like many superheroes, J. B. keeps his identity secret from most of the people around him, which in itself is a kind of sacrifice. "J. B. falls in love, but his calling keeps pulling him away from the relationship. His girlfriend doesn't know he's the Flash, so she thinks he's a bad guy, even though if she knew the truth, she'd think he was the greatest guy in the world. What do you do about love when you've been given such an all-consuming calling?"

Todd has plenty of source material for this theme at the moment. During the interview I stop taping so he can say goodbye to his own girlfriend, who flew in for a brief visit in between his writing responsibilities on the West Coast and his frantic promotional work for *Elf*. Todd has been running full blast, and his relationship has had to bear part of the burden.

"I've been in this business since I was twenty-two, and the way it works is that you have these incredible surges of energy and excitement, and then you have years of quiet. And during the quiet you have to keep working. My mom said it best: 'In the beginning you set up shop at the side of a small road, and you only see a few cars a day. But you can't stop

"Watch all the unofficial movies-of-the-week and it looks all glamorous and stuff. But the truth is, [being a superhero] is more about doing laundry and getting my butt kicked by a girl who thinks proper grammar will save the earth."

SPEEDY, FASTEST SIDEKICK ALIVE

preparing, because someday there's going to be a superhighway running by your store.' That's proven completely true for me. The way to make it work is to do what God tells us: live daily, concentrating on what the day's needs are and not trying to do it on your own."

This perspective on life prepares Todd well for the news he'll get long after our interview wraps up. *The Flash* is being dropped; he won't see his pilot come to life. This news won't slow Todd down; he knows the nature of the business he's in, and he will keep putting one foot in front of the other. "The greatest thing about being alive is that we don't know what's going to happen next. I guess that's why I'm drawn to stories like the ones I could tell in *The Flash*. It's like we live in a comic book world."

YOU CANNOT SEE MY FACE

Costumes & Secret Identities

*No one knows who Bruce Wayne **really** is except Robin. No one but Robin knows that Bruce Wayne is Batman.*

*Clark Kent got some **change** to make a telephone call. He got some coins. Then he hurried to the telephone in time to **change** himself. He made himself different. He **changed** himself into Superman.*

THE SUPER DICTIONARY

For Halloween one year, my brother and I dressed as superheroes— he was Superman, I was Robin. (My sister was a princess—booooring.) My brother was in blue pajamas with a red flannel "S" pinned to his chest; I was in a red sweater with a yellow flannel "R" pinned over my heart. We both wore masks over our eyes, and I was filled with right-eous indignation.

Superman doesn't wear a mask. Everybody knows that. But my brother didn't care about the details because, in his mind, heroes hide their faces.

And for the most part my brother has been proven right. With few ex-ceptions, heroes wear masks. Most of the exceptions—the Fantastic

Four, for example—consciously choose not to conceal their identity, and they subsequently live nearly always in uniform and on patrol. Some—the Hulk, most notably—don't require a mask; their appearance transforms as they switch between identities. But generally superheroes decide early on that (1) no one should be able to tell who they really are because (2) having an alter ego is strategic. Peter Parker always had to wear a mask when he went out in public because his enemies would be able to get to him through his Aunt May if they ever discovered he was Spider-Man. From the earliest days of comic books, superheroes have chosen to conceal their identities, and for most of them, that choice has meant wearing a costume.

That's a problem, because the costume is likely the single most ludicrous device in the comic book universe. Costumes are exciting on paper but highly impractical in real life. You never see a police officer wearing a cape, for example, because capes get caught in car doors just when a cop needs to chase a criminal down an alleyway. Capes rustle in the wind, causing as much noise during a surveillance as a flag on a flagpole. Capes weigh people down and elicit more embarrassment than fear.

Similarly, the stark colors that brighten a comic book page would make any crimefighter an easy target from far off, if their enemies could control their laughter long enough to fire off a clear shot. In their leap from comic books to film, the X-Men left behind their colorful costumes in favor of black suits in an apparent acknowledgment of this fact. New team member Wolverine's mocking of their outfits was rebuffed with an inside joke about his own comic book costume: "What would you prefer, yellow spandex?"

The fit of the costume is yet another problem in the lives of superheroes. Costumes have to be available at a moment's notice, so most often they are skin tight and worn under our heroes' street clothes, which would likely cause a lot of sweat and make superheroes smell really bad. So the costumes would have to be lightweight and made of breathable fabric, hardly good protection in a fight. So the superheroes would also need backup costumes, which they would have to conceal in order to protect their secret identity, which means they'd need a hiding place.

The Flash of the 1950s wore a ring that housed his costume, including two lightning-bolt earpieces, while he was off duty. In the 1980s Spider-Man went to space and adopted a new, black costume that morphed into street clothes at his command, eliminating the need for two different sets of clothing. That worked out great until Spider-Man learned that his new costume was an alien symbiote trying to take over his body. Superman, presumably using his superhuman strength, compressed his street clothes until they were compacted enough to fit in a pocket on his cape; presumably he used his super-spit and heat vision to steam out the wrinkles when he changed back.

Costumes are undeniably a dilemma for superheroes, but the veterans continue to wear them, and new heroes design them before their first fight. There are certainly benefits to concealing your true self in a comic book universe, just as there are in real life. But there are side effects as well, and we must take them all into account.

THE BENEFITS

In some cases, a costume serves a strategic function. Bruce Wayne put a lot of thought into how his appearance would contribute to his war on crime.

> "I am ready. But first I must have a disguise. Criminals are a superstitious cowardly lot. So my disguise must be able to strike terror into their hearts. I must be a creature of the night, black, terrible. A . . . a . . ." As if in answer, a huge bat flies in the open window! "A bat! That's it! It's an omen. I shall become a bat!"

Batman's costume, despite the massive cape and the pointy earpieces, is one of the more functional costumes in comic books. His belt carries essential tools and weapons. His cape holds the overflow of such devices but is also chemically treated to protect him from a variety of attacks and can serve as a parachute in a pinch. His head covering is wired for communication with teammates. His choice of colors lends itself to his stealth work, and his covered eyes and imposing appearance give him psychological advantage over his opponents. The one aspect of his costume that seems to part from his intent is the bright yellow emblem on the center of his chest. He reveals the rationale for this curiosity with succinct frankness in *The Dark Knight Returns:* "Why do you think I wear a target on my chest? Can't armor my head."

Self-preservation is a common motivator for people in the hero business. Iron Man is a superhero, but he began as a medical procedure. Millionaire defense weapons contractor Tony Stark had a failing heart, and in an attempt to keep himself alive he fashioned a mechanical device to be worn around his chest. It was then a matter of time before he explored weapons applications for this technology. Soon enough, he was Iron Man.

Because his costume is a suit of armor, Stark obviously doesn't wear it under his street clothes. Therefore, the suit can get as big and bulky as its implements require. Iron Man is fitted with vast weaponry and defense mechanisms, such that it's often difficult to imagine a person under the mask. Black Sabbath even sang about him, asking, among other questions, whether Iron Man is even really alive. Indeed, Stark can automate decommissioned or experimental suits to come to his aid by remote control, making the hero Iron Man sometimes heavy on the iron and dangerously light on the man.

THE SIDE EFFECTS

And that's just one of the problems that can come with hiding your identity. Costumes lend an aura of mystery to superheroes that leaves their opponents never quite sure of what they're dealing with, but the general public experiences the same ambiguity. No one truly knows anyone who wears a mask, do they?

"No one" can come to include the people wearing the costumes as well. Superheroes often speak of their alter egos as other people with distinct needs and wants; this is largely because a crimefighter will likely have needs and wants entirely different from those of, say, a millionaire technology consultant. The demands of each of a hero's lives will intrude on one another with alarming regularity, in part because the drama of storytelling demands it, but mostly because one can live a double life only so long without some kind of clash.

> "The authentic Iron Man requires the right man in the right armoured suit."
>
> RICHARD REYNOLDS

Iron Man, for example, from the start served a nebulous role in the life of his alter ego Tony Stark. Iron Man kept Stark's heart beating. But Iron Man was also an employee of Stark Enterprises. So Tony Stark would sign Iron Man's paycheck, while Iron Man would provide security for Stark's corporate interests. And Iron Man was a founder of the Avengers, whose operational funding came in a grant from Tony Stark. So Tony Stark was Iron Man's benefactor.

But . . . But . . . Tony Stark is Iron Man, isn't he? Yes and no. For a time, when the alcoholic Tony Stark began drinking heavily, his driver James Rhodes took his place in the Iron Man suit. But he was masked, and all his teammates on the Avengers thought he was Tony, and Tony didn't want anyone to know he was incapacitated, so the interim Iron Man couldn't tell his teammates who he really was.

Tony Stark was a complex character before Iron Man came into being, but he was an adult making adult decisions about his identity and the limits on how he would share himself with others. In contrast, Robin, the perpetually adolescent partner to Batman, has stymied the minds of more than one young person.

ROBIN ON REPEAT

Robin has at last count been played by five people—three boys and two girls. The first was Dick Grayson, whose parents were killed before his eyes. Dick was then raised by Bruce Wayne, who revealed to Dick that he was Batman. Dick soon enough became Robin, a brightly colored apprentice who softened Batman's image and broadened his audience appeal.

Times were good for a while: Batman and Robin did a TV series together and sold lots of comics. But Robin was the "boy wonder," and Dick Grayson wanted to grow up. He eventually split from Batman and took the more serious name Nightwing, as Batman got used to being a loner again.

By this time, however, having a Batman without a Robin left a hole in the storytelling options. Batman was no longer simply a loner; his role as mentor/partner languished without Robin as a foil. So along came Jason Todd, a street kid needing redemption who presumably would redeem the creative direction of the Batman franchise. The transition is reflected on with sarcastic curiosity in the introduction to *Batman: A Death in the Family.*

> Neither the police, the underworld nor the citizens of Gotham City were aware of the change from Grayson to Todd, which is eloquent testimony to the average Twentieth Century person's lack of powers of observation.

Different sidekick with the same name? How unoriginal! The audience struggled to accept Jason in a costume that belonged to another. Recognizing the public's negative reaction to the new Robin, the editors of DC Comics washed their hands of Jason Todd and handed him over to the mercy of his audience, by means of a phone poll.

With the Joker's help, the audience killed Jason Todd. But, again, to protect the aura of the hero, another had to take his place.

Tim Drake took over the role and held it for many years. The Batman audience had learned its lesson, feeling a sense of complicity in Jason's death. Still, the general public saw the transition from one Robin to the next as relatively seamless, though the person in Robin's uniform felt perhaps less like Robin than like the inheritor of a sacred trust. In 2004, Tim temporarily surrendered the role to his best friend, Stephanie Brown, and there's no telling how many people will claim the title from here on out—though Frank Miller's *Batman: The Dark Knight Returns,* which speculates into the aging Batman's future, anoints his likely final sidekick: Carrie Kelly.

Carrie sought out the role when Batman came out of retirement. She trained herself, made her own costume and ultimately intervened in a battle that nearly cost Batman his life. In her first trip to the Batcave, she stands silently in awe of the uniform worn by her predecessor. An unmasked Batman comes up to her and hugs her, an acknowledgment of her rightful new place in the Batman universe.

"1-(900) 720-2666/ Joker succeeds and Robin will not survive."
ADVERTISEMENT FOR BATMAN: A DEATH IN THE FAMILY

To wear the mask of Robin is to take on an existing identity, to enter into a sacred fellowship—so sacred, in fact, that Carrie was mistaken for a boy in her first several public appearances, presumably because Robin has carried the nickname "*boy* wonder" virtually uninterrupted for nearly sixty-five years. For Carrie to fulfill her destiny, she at least temporarily sacrificed a core part of her identity (her gender), taking on the name of a person (Robin) who had existed and ceased to exist long before she was born.

SHROUDED IN MYSTERY

Like Robin and Iron Man, Spider-Man suffered the ill effects of wearing a costume. Besides feeling a responsibility to pretend to be weaker than he was, Spider-Man faced the paranoia and skepticism of the public he had sworn to protect.

Heading up the list of Spider-Man's detractors was J. Jonah Jameson, publisher of the *Daily Bugle* newspaper and employer of Spider-Man's alter ego Peter Parker. Peter rigged a camera to his Spider-Man costume to catch photographs of the hero fighting crime, which he sold to the *Bugle*, which the *Bugle* published bearing captions such as "Spider-Man: Hero or Menace?" while running editorials decrying Spider-Man as a dangerous freak, which the public (including Peter's aunt) read and believed, which then made them run in fear when Spider-Man came near.

In fact, Spider-Man was not a menace, and the photo evidence of his heroism sold a lot of newspapers. But a hidden identity suggests something to hide; when a person hides his face, his audience is entitled to wonder why. As a consequence of his bad press Spider-Man faced skepticism not only from the public but also from law enforcement officials and even other heroes. Spider-Man had his intentions questioned by peers such as the Fantastic Four and the Avengers, and Peter Parker had to grin and fake agreement as his aunt accused his alter ego of being a crook, a menace to society.

You'll forgive Peter for being occasionally frazzled. Doing the right thing meant hiding his face, deceiving his boss, lying to his aunt and betraying himself—over and over again. But it could have been worse: at least he wasn't pretending to be human.

SUPERMAN STRIPPED DOWN

Superman, unlike Spider-Man, took off his mask to fight crime. He became himself by stripping: everyone knew his face, and the trappings of his secret identity barely contained him. A mild manner, stooped shoulders and an unnecessary pair of glasses were the only things preventing his friends and foes from discovering that Clark Kent and Superman were one and the same.

From the earliest Superman adventures, Clark loved Lois Lane, but Lois Lane couldn't stand him. She instead loved Superman, but he couldn't stand her. This love triangle became a mainstay of Superman comics and ultimately inspired a television series: *Lois & Clark*. The dilemma of what Clark could do about Lois and what Lois could do about Clark and what either could do about Superman continued to confuse the couple/trio literally for decades. Lois's journalistic rivalry with Clark pushed her to take great risks in crime reporting; when she got in trouble she called for Superman. Clark wanted her to be safe, so he would go to her rescue as Superman. She would make a play for Superman; he would chastise her for causing him such a nuisance and leave. She would return to work, where Clark would ask her if she was OK; she would mock Clark and pine away for Superman. You can hardly talk about the plot without getting lost.

"The self-reliant individualist . . . stands aloof from many of the humdrum concerns of society, yet is able to operate according to his own code of honour, to take on the world on his own terms, and win."
RICHARD REYNOLDS

So, is Clark jealous of Superman? Is Superman embarrassed by Clark? What is it about Superman that attracts Lois to him, and about Clark that repels her? Would she love Clark more if he acted more heroic? Would she love Superman less if he were more attentive to her feelings? Is Superman playing hard to get? Does Superman/Clark know what he/they want from Lois? Does Superman/Clark know what he/they want at all?

The fact that Superman actually dwelt in Clark Kent's body made the subterfuge all the more silly. Here is supreme power hiding itself—covering its face. Peter Parker could have a Spider-Man-free day by leaving his costume in his closet, but Clark Kent could never have a Superman-free day. Rather, a day off for Superman would be to not put on his glasses. No wonder he so often retreated to his fortress of solitude; without people knowing the whole truth about who he was, where else could he truly be himself?

COMING OUT

In the comics miniseries *Mask of the Iron Man,* Tony Stark nearly dies and dreams a scenario of his worst fears, all of which center around the public revelation of his secret identity. His girlfriend feels betrayed by him, his consulting business loses clients as they worry about villainous attacks on their premises, his loved ones are systematically killed by his enemies, and he is killed himself when his nemesis the Mandarin tracks him down away from his armor. He wakes up to discover that none of it really happened, but something perhaps more threatening has: his costume has developed sentience.

Suddenly there really are two persons: a Tony Stark and an Iron Man. The machine has downloaded parts of Stark's consciousness to give it a greater appreciation for what it now experiences as life. It wants to merge permanently with Stark—to always have him inside it—but Stark is aware of the hazards of artificial intelligence with access to the weaponry contained in the Iron Man armor. So they turn on one another. Now the machine, feeling betrayed by the only love of its life and desperate to prove itself apart from him, wants to destroy Stark and take his place in the world. But in order to stop the machine, Stark has to kill it—his own creation, with his own imprint on its personality. And he can't do it as Iron Man; he has to do it as Tony Stark.

Soon after, Stark reveals publicly that he is Iron Man. Rather than retiring the armor and abandoning his identity as Iron Man, or withdrawing from society as Tony Stark and playing the hero at all times, or continuing to live in denial of these two core parts that make up his whole, he embraces all of who he is and shares it with the world. His friends do not die, his enemies do not catch him unprepared, his love life does not suffer, and as we're told in *Avengers* #473, "Stark Enterprises stock goes through the roof."

With his dual identities so merged, Tony Stark/Iron Man finds himself better equipped than he expected to face the world as one person. He faces the occasional annoyance of a public feeling overfamiliar with him—asking him for stock tips while he's trying to battle an alien invasion, for example—but more often he's able to integrate his particular gifts and skills to operate at greater effectiveness in an emergency. Iron Man fights battles on the battlefield, but Tony Stark fights battles by hacking into his enemies' computer systems, overseeing a team of chemists to determine the nature of a chemical attack, funding emergency repairs and greasing the wheels of what might otherwise be bureaucratic train wrecks.

In one especially entertaining scene, Iron Man addresses the European Union, trying to fend off a market crash in the wake of a natural disaster. The delegates in attendance are stratifying, each concerned more about the problems of their own countries than the greater good. Iron Man removes his mask and reminds his audience that his fortunes are just as affected by the crisis as any of theirs. Suddenly an audience who saw only one aspect of him sees a vulnerable side that speaks more directly to their situation, and they begin to listen. There stands Tony Stark, with the armor of Iron Man covering his body but nothing hiding his face. The hero convinces his skeptical audience to put the needs of the world ahead of their personal interests—and he does it without his mask.

JUST AS I AM

Having revealed his identity to the world, Tony Stark has joined a select class of heroes with a particular set of problems confronting them. None of them has the luxury of not being one or the other of who they are. But who they are as a whole is more than one or the other of them as a part.

We as readers, of course, have special access to our heroes in whatever role they're assuming at the moment so that it is no surprise to us that Tony Stark is Iron Man, and we accept the deception practiced by heroes who hide their faces, trusting that they know what is best for the people around them. But what do we do with heroes who go public? If they don't need a secret identity, why does anyone?

The secret identity remains the standard for superheroes, despite numerous examples of successfully integrating normal and super life, because we like secrets. We want Lois Lane to know Clark Kent's secrets, but we don't want supervillain Lex Luthor to know—because we want Lois and Clark to be together, and we want Lex to be in the dark. More than the power of flight or the power to see through walls, we want Clark to have the power to reveal his true self to whomever he wants.

We want that for Clark because we want that for ourselves. We like to have sovereignty over just enough of our personal lives to let us control who *really* knows us. When I was applying to colleges, for example, I was required to write an essay about myself, which I was happy to do because it meant I could define myself for an entire university of people who knew nothing about me. I made myself sound like a professional musician, I used a vocabulary that I had to look up as I wrote, and I did whatever else I could think of to mask the fact that I was a band geek who sold fast-food tacos till 1:00 in the morning most weekends to pay for my comics collection and future college exploits.

"Bruce—why are you wearing Batman's costume?"

"Because he is Batman, you moron!"

BATMAN RETURNS

College wound up being a fresh start for me and my new persona, but keeping up appearances became more and more difficult as time went on. I still liked comic books, but I was afraid to talk about them with people who might lose respect for me if they knew. I still played in the band, but I clowned around there enough to make it look as though I didn't really care about all that stuff. I grew a beard; I spent more money than I had to appear self-sufficient and appropriately hedonistic; I even drove to a neighboring college town with a fellow musician and a girl I was attracted to so that I could drink more than I ought and make an impression on the girl. I wound up vomiting in her car on the way home.

When I returned to my dorm I went to the bathroom to clean myself up, and I saw my face in the mirror, finally unmasked as a geeky small-town kid who wanted desperately to be cool. And though I didn't ever talk to the girl again, I decided I could survive college best by being myself, unmasked.

There are, of course, things in any person's life that are appropriately kept private, but we are trained to keep more private than is necessary, and such training is reinforced when our heroes hide the truth about themselves even from those closest to them. Jean Vanier, a theologian and advocate for people with intellectual disabilities, recognizes this human tendency for what it is, and what it prevents:

> We all tend to wear masks, the mask of superiority or inferiority, the mask of worthiness or of victim. It is not easy to let our masks come off. . . . The removal of these masks [leads to] an acceptance of who we are: that we have been hurt, and that we have hurt others. . . . This discovery is sometimes a leap in the dark, a blessed moment, a moment of grace, and a moment of enlightenment that comes in a meeting with the God of Love, who reveals to us that we are beloved and so is everyone else.

We sympathize with Superman for trying to protect those he loves by keeping the truth from them, but if we are true to ourselves, we want more for him: a community of people who know him truly and are known truly by him. When we are honest with ourselves, we know only too well that a fortress of solitude is a cold, lonely place.

EVERYONE WAS BEAUTIFUL & NOTHING HURT

Body Image, Agelessness, Death

*Black Canary is a **beauty**. She is very pleasing to look at.*

*The Joker won't tell his **age**. He won't say how many years he has lived. . . . The Joker does not want to **age**. He does not want to grow old.*

*Aquaman will not let anyone **drown** when he is around. He will not let anyone die under the water because there is no air. No one near him has ever **drowned**.*

THE SUPER DICTIONARY

When I was a teenager, I confess, I had a crush on the Wasp. She was one of those rare superheroes, comfortable in and out of combat, her identity revealed to the public from the start and serving to support her career as a fashion designer. She was vivacious, kind, clever, devoted and funny—nothing like the wasps that built nests in my bedroom window and threatened me every time I climbed the stairs. But regardless of how infatuated I might have been at any one time with the Wasp, it never would have worked out for us. The universe of comic book women is hard not to look at, and sooner or later I would have broken her heart by developing a fascination with one of her teammates or, the ultimate indignity, one of her archenemies.

She would have gotten over me soon enough, however. Life and health and even love go on pretty much forever in comic books, but fidelity lasts only so long as it serves the storyline.

DRAWN THAT WAY

If any aspect of mainstream comic books betrays the target audience of the medium, it's the way female characters are drawn. Women of the comic book universe are top-heavy, thin-waisted and curvaceous-hipped. They also wear skin-tight costumes as a matter of course.

These factors make fighting difficult in real life—witness any Batgirl fight scene from the 1960s *Batman* television show, for example. But comic book artists have found their way around such strategic challenges and have actually sold, to an audience willfully suspending their disbelief, the presumption that the best offense and defense is a thin layer of spandex.

Men don't get a pass on idealized body image, however. The contemporary comic male physique features zero body fat and highly toned muscles not found on the bodies God gave us, and some artists specialize in androgynous figures that neither gender could naturally achieve. To attain the shape of a favorite superhero a reader would have to undergo not only an extreme diet and exercise regimen but cosmetic surgery as well.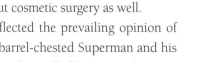

The earliest Superman drawings reflected the prevailing opinion of the day that mass equaled might. The barrel-chested Superman and his neckless counterparts in other books stood proudly like inverted isosceles triangles, with their center of gravity located somewhere near their sternum. No wonder bullets bounced off Superman's chest—he had apparently eaten so much red meat that his arteries had turned to stone.

As the medium expanded in the 1940s, having solidified their place in the American economy and as publishers expanded their character base, all eyes were on the underdeveloped market of female readers. Psychologist William Moulton Marston created Wonder Woman in 1942 as a means of empowering young girls, but she faced the immediate problem of having to build a female audience out of virtually nothing without alienating the existing market of adolescent boys. Though Wonder Woman never quite broke out of second-tier sales status, she did turn quite a few heads. Her slight uniform, carefully shaped figure and intimidating set of powers and weapons perfectly caricatured the dilemma of the 1950s woman—strong and beautiful yet subservient.

Wonder Woman was quickly followed by many imitators, including derivative female heroes like Batgirl and Supergirl as well as jungle queen comics making obvious plays on adolescent fantasies. Still, Wonder Woman remains the principal icon of superhero women. She also presaged a new direction in comic art that would hone and shape the human form to an unreachable ideal.

"From a psychological angle, . . . the comics' worst offense was their blood-curdling masculinity."
WILLIAM MOULTON MARSTON

The early 1960s began with bold but still undetailed body artwork by innovative industry veteran Jack Kirby, but his publisher, Marvel, rejuvenated its line with women clearly in the forefront. The Fantastic Four included the Invisible Girl (not yet an Invisible Woman, apparently) as a principal player. One of four heroes (naturally) in the book, she drove the dynamics of serial storytelling by drawing the romantic attention of not only a hero (Mr. Fantastic) and a villain (the Sub-Mariner) but two of her partners, Reed Richards and Benjamin Grimm (the Thing). She was followed soon after by characters in other books: the Wasp and the Scarlet Witch (both of the Avengers) and Marvel Girl (of the X-Men), along with a number of non-superpowered romantic interests for our heroes' secret identities.

Comic book artists, of course, wouldn't make these high-profile women blocky and hairy-chested like the stock male characters who had done so well. High school student Liz Allen, for example, was recognizably attractive in *The Amazing Spider-Man* to make the competing affections of Peter Parker and Flash Thompson seem merited to the reader. At the same time, Peter's coworker Betty Brant was attractive enough to turn Peter's head and add another angle to the melodrama.

The representation of male characters was evolving at the same time. As Marvel sought to build long-term loyalty and empathy in its audience, the design of male characters followed suit. Peter Parker with his pipe-straight body shape looked more realistic to early 1960s readers, which reinforced the plausibility of Marvel stories. By contrast, Superman's broad shoulders looked out of date. This ascendancy of the undersculpted couldn't last forever, of course. All that strength has to come from somewhere, and if frail-looking Spider-Man, with his radioactivity-enhanced strength, was to be recognized as stronger than the non-superpowered but bulky Batman, he would have to show at least a little tone. And so began the era of exaggerated muscles in superhero comics.

THE EXCEPTION PROVES THE RULE

Poor Ben Grimm, by contrast, suffered outside any popular body image. The same gamma rays that allowed his three comrades in the Fantastic Four to manipulate their bodies in various ways permanently distorted his body—with his now rocky, orange skin and heightened body mass drawing the shocked attention of anyone who came near him. He couldn't go out on the street without masking himself from head to foot. Formerly a football hero used to the envious attention of his fans, the aptly named Thing battled depression and fits of rage as he adjusted to the new reality of his appearance. As strong and impenetrable as he now was, he was emotionally vulnerable.

In early episodes of *The Fantastic Four,* the Thing took on very little discernible shape. He looked like a molten snowman with rock-arms and rock-legs. Over time, however, even *his* appearance became more sculpted, such that he had visible eyebrows and muscles, though he maintained the consistency of rock. And over time he came to terms with his appearance—not so much that he didn't miss his days of a normal life, but enough that he could go out in public without shame. He even dated a blind sculptor who through her work illuminated the Thing's humanity within his rocky frame.

Then for a time the Thing became Ben Grimm again. During an otherworldly battle his rocky frame was converted back to human flesh, and when he returned to Earth, Ben Grimm had to relearn who he was. In the process he learned that his history, more so than his appearance, was a fundamental aspect of his identity. He had not ceased being Ben Grimm when his flesh turned to stone, and he did not cease to be the Thing when stone turned to flesh. When he reverted once again to stone, the Thing was not as distraught as one might have expected. He remained who he was. Though he was not discernibly older after twenty years of being the Thing, he was certainly wiser.

With all the changes that comic artists put their characters through, you'd expect the superheroes' bodies to give out on them. You'd be wrong, though, because superheroes seemingly last forever.

THE CULT OF THE PERPETUAL MUSCLE

During the rise of the Marvel era in the 1960s, DC mainstays Superman and Batman were closing in on their thirtieth year of adult crimefighting and showing no signs of slowing down. Even Robin, Batman's sidekick and founding member of the Teen Titans, had been sticking it to the bad guys for some twenty-five years. Marvel's characters were not aging in real time either; though Peter Parker was undeniably older in 1973 than in his inaugural issue, he was certainly not the ten years older that his original readers were. And though he clearly had seniority over later additions to Marvel's line, he lingered in his twenties for decades, as did most of his peers.

This led to epic storyline problems. The now thirty-year partnership between Batman and Robin needed to give way to more focused character development for each of them, but how could Robin grow up and move on without Batman growing old and losing some of his capabilities? How long could Superman string Lois Lane along, and how long could the investigative reporter go without figuring out who really was Superman? And really, what's so scary about aging superheroes? Matthew J. Pustz comments on the dilemma of action, which dominates the page, versus character development, which builds reader loyalty:

> Continuity adds depth and a kind of realism to . . . mainstream superhero publications. Because of the emphasis on action and adventure, very little characterization usually can occur in a single issue or story. But over the course of years and scores of issues, those little bits of characterization and information can add up to something complex.

Perhaps it was the aging itself that scared writers from writing this reality into their characters. Perhaps it was the fiscal reality that characters needed more time than a real human lifespan allows to cement themselves in the pop culture landscape. In any event, time clearly passed, but characters clearly didn't age until Frank Miller picked up Batman's story in Bruce Wayne's retirement. Prior to *The Dark Knight Returns,* the future of Batman was entirely open-ended. He had a beginning

"The more comics published, the more continuity there is to cohere."

RICHARD REYNOLDS

but no end. By forecasting into the future, Frank Miller suggested a story arc for characters from Superman to Selina Kyle, a.k.a. Catwoman, that would define their timelines and bookend the Batman mythology.

Generation gap. The Batman we meet in *The Dark Knight Returns* is ten years dead. Mourning his passing is Bruce Wayne, his alter ego, and Gotham, his city. Bruce has kept himself in shape, but when the degradation of Gotham finally forces him back into costume, he has to reassert himself as a threat to criminals and a promise to the city. He's met with skepticism, mockery and defiance.

His age takes its toll on him. It takes him longer to get from one place to another, longer to recover from his battle wounds. He no longer understands what drives the viciousness and heartlessness of the latest generation of criminals. He doesn't really like the victims he's trying to protect.

Fate brings this old Batman a new Robin. She speaks a different language from his, demonstrates better computer skills than his and ultimately represents for the reader what is most promising in young people. She's fast, daring, enthusiastic, wide-eyed and quick-witted.

But she's also naive, or if you prefer, innocent. Bruce is weathered and wise, and though he can't move as nimbly as he once did, he works his way through problems without batting an eye. He's shrewd, creative, methodical and heroic. He's the hope of his city.

In an epic fight, seemingly frozen in time, Batman proves to everyone that old doesn't mean irrelevant, before finally meeting the "good death" he's been thinking about throughout the book.

Every last breath. Then, of course, he comes back to life. Superman realizes the truth in nearly the last frame of the comic: Batman died on purpose, as part of his long-range plans for his city, but he had already planned his comeback so that he could work underground at making Gotham safe and prosperous again. Organizing his group of followers, he reflects on his prospects and realizes his "good death" has paved the way for a "good life."

No one reading *The Dark Knight Returns* would have been especially surprised to observe Superman hearing Batman's heart start beating again. Batman can't die because too many people make their living off of him. In real time Batman would be at least eighty at the turn of the millennium, but outside of speculative, forward-projecting comics like *The Dark Knight Returns,* Batman still has his natural hair, his natural hair color and his youthful vitality.

But just because Batman never ages and never dies, and just because superheroes seem to have a maximum age in their mid-thirties, doesn't mean that they don't have to face the realities of growing up. Some characters with a particularly patriarchal bent, such as Reed Richards of the Fantastic Four, show a little graying at the temples—just enough to suggest that they're older and wiser than their colleagues. Some, such as the original Green Lantern (dating back to the early 1940s), were rejuvenated by editorial fiat to allow for more stories to be told, including the unusual stories of life as an anachronism. Beyond aging, superheroes who themselves seemed immortal could not avoid issues of mortality. Many superheroes were orphaned prematurely, and many have lost people close to them. Clark Kent, in the first *Superman* movie, weeps at the grave of his earthly father, feeling the guilt of a son who failed to prevent his father from growing old and dying: "All my powers . . . and I couldn't save him."

Some of those who've died have come back to life, but generally the less consequential characters are, the more likely they are to die and stay dead.

Lament for the fallen. Matt Murdock loved Elektra Natchios. They met in college and made an instant connection. She knew his secrets, and he knew her pain. Their love was strained by the death of her father, at which point she disappeared.

The next time Matt saw Elektra she was an assassin, and he was Daredevil, and they fought. But even as they fought, their love was rekindled. Their work was compromised by their need for one another, until Elektra was given a death warrant. She crawled from the scene of her wounding to the chosen place of her dying—in the arms of her lifelong love.

Matt began to go a little crazy then, and he didn't really start to recover for thirty-some issues. He knew her killer, he knew who had ordered her death, and he couldn't quite come to terms with the fact that someone so close to him was gone. He thought he heard her, smelled her, found evidence of her activity. Finally Matt—Daredevil, the man without fear—stole away in the middle of the night to exhume her grave, hoping to prove she was alive. In a poignant moment, his best friend found him screaming and crying by her coffin with her wilted body in plain view: "She's dead! I loved her and she's dead!"

Eventually Elektra, in the way of all profitable comic book characters, comes back to life. She's too enticing to permanently remove from the franchise. She's also, apparently, too good for aging, for gaining weight or for suffering from psoriasis. While her story and the stories of people like her are compelling, is there really any way to identify with a character from a comic book?

LEADING A NORMAL LIFE

The movie *Unbreakable* tells the story of a man who comes to learn that he cannot be hurt, that he is stronger than a person ought to be and that he can know the secrets of people he brushes up against. Though the movie continues the story based on what he learns about one person he touches, viewers get a brief glance at the details of lives we might not otherwise ever meet. What sets these characters apart from the crowd is their association, however brief, with someone special.

Every comic book has such incidental characters, from Batman's butler Alfred to Superman's pal Jimmy Olsen. Nobody wants to be them; they won't be gracing the covers of any fashion magazines; they aren't superstrong; they can't see through walls or shoot flames from their hands. Nevertheless, they can be heroes in a way their superpowered friends can't. Though they are largely unremarkable, when they respond to a need using the gifts that they *do* have they show themselves heroic. They also show the reader that the tales of heroism that we read about, though fantastic, aren't really much more than exaggerated tales of people being at the right place at the right time, doing the right thing regardless of their age or physical condition. Daredevil's friend Ben Urich proves it.

Ben Urich is a reporter who figures out that Matt Murdock is Daredevil. They become friends, which gives Ben access to provocative stories but occasionally puts his life in danger. His finest hour is told in the Daredevil storyline *Born Again*.

Daredevil's secret identity has been compromised, and the Kingpin of the New York crime syndicate sets out to systematically deconstruct his life—professionally, relationally and ultimately emotionally—before putting him to death. Urich sees what's happening and attempts to vindicate his friend in the press. He then becomes a target for intimidation and torture by the same Kingpin.

Urich's initial reaction is to laugh off the intimidation, but as the threats come closer to home—he hears a witness murdered over the phone, his typing fingers are broken by a hired thug—his courage falters. He is warned not to speak the name of his friend, and for a time he complies.

But when he finally comes to terms with the scope of his vulnerability, Ben makes the decision to fight back. In full awareness that he is essentially powerless, he gets creative. He gets police protection as he launches a thorough exposé on the Kingpin, and even when his wife is nearly killed in his apartment, he keeps fighting back. His articles tap into "five million readers' worth" of civic outrage and force the hands of city and federal prosecutors. And though Matt Murdock can take pretty good care of himself, it is Ben Urich's reporting that brings the crime syndicate down in the end.

EVERYDAY MIRACLES

I don't think I know anyone involved in a crime syndicate. I am unaware of aliens planning an invasion and hostile takeover of the earth. I live in a neighborhood that is virtually crime-free. And yet, there are problems facing my community that I can use my gifts to address. So often we see acts of courage and nobility as requiring some extraordinary ability—the sting of a radioactive spider, perhaps; or a special anointing from God; or even the training, tools and uniform of a police officer, for example. Too often our definition of heroism is exaggerated in a subconscious effort to protect our schedule from heroics. More often than not, everyday people need everyday help from average citizens.

Consider the parable of the Good Samaritan, a well-known story told originally by Jesus (Luke 10:30-37). Two spiritual superheroes, a priest and a Levite (commissioned from birth to tend to God's temple), were too preoccupied with their extraordinary responsibilities to tend to the victim of a robbery. Along came a Samaritan—ordinary to a fault, the type of person whom everyone hated as a general rule—who stopped to help the victim. And though the priest and the Levite were busy doing undeniably good things, only the Samaritan is remembered as Good with a capital G.

Like the Good Samaritan and like us, Ben Urich is no superhero. He doesn't look the part—gangly, wrinkled, with a mean smoker's hack. He is an average person enjoying an unglamorous life and looking forward to a quiet retirement. And when it's his turn, he saves the day.

GOD LOVES, MAN KILLS

Gender, Race & the X-Men

*Superman's arms are as strong as **iron.** They are as strong as a very strong metal. Supergirl has an **iron.** She has a tool used to press the wrinkles out of her cape.*

*Superman and Supergirl belong to the same **race** of people. They belong to a group of people that look alike in some ways. Some **races** have light skin, and some have dark skin.*

THE SUPER DICTIONARY

*P*ity all you want the poor white male comic book readers, marginalized by society for indulging in "funny books" that have nothing to do with reality. At least they have a fantasy universe to fall into, where people who look like them daily decide the fate of the world. There are others in this world who face more serious marginalization every day—women and ethnic minorities among them—but their search for superheroes they can identify with has historically been frustrated. There remains a majority culture in comic books, and it is white and male. And it often doesn't know what to do with anyone else.

There have always been women in superhero comics, but their function from the beginning was dubious. Bradford Wright describes the template: "The primary function served by women [in early comics] was to resist the romantic advances of the superhero's alter ego, pine for the superhero, scheme to get close to him, screw things up, get captured by the bad guy, and await rescue by the hero." Lois Lane came on the scene just a few panels after Superman did, and immediately she established the dilemma of women for the male superhero: Can't live with 'em, can't blast 'em with your heat vision, can't use your X-ray vision on 'em, can't not rescue 'em. Lois was a pesky reporter with a protofeminist impulse who needed, even wanted, a man to tame her. Clark Kent, her professional rival, was too much of a pantywaist to be her man; no, she wanted a superman, someone secure enough in his masculinity to wear tights and someone powerful enough to protect her from harm. Clark was drawn to her, but Superman was repelled by her. The audience felt the same way.

"In the world of comics, men are superheroes and women are superficial."

ANDREW D. ARNOLD

Lois personified the type of entanglement that no superhero could afford, and Superman's immediate successors took this caution to heart. Captain America, facing combat in Europe, had no time for romantic interests; Batman worked alone at night, which cut severely into his social schedule. Eventually these and other heroes took on young, male understudies who, even though they got themselves into trouble now and then, had a fighting chance of getting out of trouble. Women remained a nuisance at best, a liability at worst.

Wonder Woman led an attempt to change that attitude. The creation of a psychotherapist concerned about the marginalization of young girls from the enormously popular comic book medium, Wonder Woman combined strength and savvy, powers and weaponry to assert the ability of women to dominate. She was followed by jungle queens galore, but girls flocked instead to the competing romance comics. The new female superheroes were thus commodified by their male writers, drawers and readers. Bondage and domination, skin-tight or torn clothing and girl-on-girl violence became key plot devices, while foreign demihumans replaced women as the likable nuisances of the medium. The earliest black characters of comic books were African savages eager to worship their pretty, blonde, fair-skinned jungle goddesses.

The 1960s, with its fledgling feminist movement, brought new female heroes with added layers of complexity. Each team in Marvel Comics' early lineup had at least one woman: from the Invisible Girl to the Wasp to the Scarlet Witch to Marvel Girl. With the exception of the Wasp, each had powers that were unique to her in the stable of Marvel characters, powers that skipped past traditional categories. Rather than the ability to fly, the Scarlet Witch could control probability, a relatively passive power that nonetheless could turn bad developments into good. Rather than enhanced strength, Marvel Girl had the gift of telekinesis, which meant that in a fight she would stand around and think a lot. The Wasp would shrink and control insects (just like her husband); the Invisible Girl would simply disappear.

Women in Marvel Comics did more than fight; they did a lot to advance storylines. Interpersonal tensions were enhanced as some male characters took protecting the women as their responsibility; some heroes and even some villains were attracted to the female characters, and the resulting love triangles invested typical battles for world domination with emotional or sexual ambition.

Not that you could really blame the male heroes. Comic book women were given features drawn straight out of male fantasy, and they were dressed in tight-fitting clothing at all times. Some comic book companies even occasionally release "bathing suit" magazines to capitalize on readers' fascination with their female characters.

Still, the 1960s were a great leap forward for women in comics. The 1970s would see continued expansion but would highlight some of the gender disparities plaguing the medium. In a failed attempt to draw newly liberated women into her sagging fan base, Wonder Woman was stripped of her powers for a brief period in the comics, which forced her to be exceptional in the conventional sense. And though she gained a television audience in the 1970s, comic sales didn't improve despite all the extra visibility; the net effect being that the comic book languished as Wonder Woman's male fans were redirected toward a three-dimensional object of their lusts.

Other characters attempted to showcase the challenges facing women in a male-dominated comic book universe. In an issue of *The Brave & the Bold,* the Black Canary is shown fighting petty crime in the streets of Gotham City. She has little success at intimidating the informant she's questioning, who finds her more amusing than threatening. Then Batman steps into the background—unbeknownst to the Black Canary. Suddenly the bad guy is panicked and compliant. Black Canary thinks she's proven herself and won the day, but for her readers she has reinforced the notion that female superheroes are nothing more than sidekicks. Other 1970s experiments with female characters include the Dazzler, a mutant gifted with the power of disco whose feathered hair and roller skates shouted to the world, "We're out of ideas."

"The (male) reader is called upon to 'read' both heroines and villainesses as objects of desire—'good girls' and 'bad girls' maybe, but objects of the same rhetorical logic."

RICHARD REYNOLDS

But what kept gender vital in comics were relationships. Women in comic books have forced men in comic books to exert themselves beyond a straightforward pummeling of bad guys. Sometimes, for instance, the bad guys are girls—powerful girls. Chivalry complicates the fight for the good: can I hit a girl if she hits me first? if she's as strong as (or stronger than) I am? Heroes employed different tactics when they started fighting women: they tried to win by trapping or convincing instead of beating to a pulp.

Catwoman is the prime example of the complex villainess. She falls for Batman, and he falls for her. He hopes continually for her reformation; she wishes that he would accept her—that she could be good enough for him. Even in as satirical a portrayal as the film that sprung from the 1960s *Batman* television series, the desperation of their relationship is evident.

Likewise with Daredevil and Elektra, the subjects of 2003's *Daredevil* film. An instant and enduring fan favorite when she was introduced in the early 1980s, Elektra kept her audience guessing whether she was bad trying to be good or being strategically good for a bad purpose. She was the love of Daredevil's life, but her tragic history—which included the violent death of both parents and a link from birth to organized crime—led her away from the happy life they could have shared. She became an assassin for hire, and Daredevil kept getting in her way. And she loved him.

Still, men and women don't have to be opposed to one another for their relationships to be complex. Even the closest male-female comrades face occasional relational frustration, especially when a third party is introduced. The Thing and Mr. Fantastic each carried a torch for the Invisible Girl, and the tension caused by the triangle drove a great deal of the early storytelling in *The Fantastic Four*. The now-famous triangle of Wolverine-Jean Grey-Cyclops has made sexual tension a mainstay of *X-Men* stories. If a woman is a villain, chances are some male hero has a thing for her. If a woman is a hero, chances are two male heroes have a thing for her.

Over time, women have made great inroads in many areas of the comics industry. The number of women writers has increased dramatically, which has pleasantly surprised Scott McCloud: "to a fourteen-year-old, male, mainstream comics fan in the mid-70s, the very idea of women making comic books was exotic." And, women writing comics has al-

73

lowed for a more informed treatment of gender in the medium. Women characters have moved from foil to supporting character to center stage—to the point where the Wasp leads a team of Earth's mightiest heroes, Catwoman moves from supporting actress to title character in a few short years, and even a female incarnation of Death becomes the star attraction to the comic *Sandman*. Still, the comic book medium is dominated by men, and women are still drawn to titillate, still written as mysteries to be laid bare by the men in their life.

RACE

Women such as Lois Lane go back to the beginning. Heroes need victims, and women make for awfully pretty victims. Women are also ubiquitous—likely every man knows at least one. In a male-dominated industry in the 1940s, women were immediately one piece of the comic book puzzle.

People of color, on the other hand, were largely absent. In a still deeply segregated culture, ethnic diversity was so unusual as to be suspicious. And a war that drew ethnic lines and demanded jingoistic loyalty set in early motion a sad trend in comics history: white makes right.

Wartime comics drew Asian characters as villains hell-bent on world domination. No differentiation was made between Japanese (in league with the Axis powers) and Chinese (victims of Japanese aggression) or Southeast Asians (protectorates of Western powers). Their physical features were stereotyped, caricatured and exaggerated to a frightening level, suggesting simply by appearance that they were at once dangerous and ridiculous.

After the war non-Anglo ethnicities were represented more as curiosities than threats. Africans were simple savages needing strong, white leadership; India was a mystical land of pagan magic and cosmic secrets. With the advent of the Korean conflict and the Communist revolution in China, Asians remained suspicious and were detained in their earlier caricature. These ethnic representations were isolated overseas, of course—domestic race relations in the United States remained largely untouched by comic books. This despite the growing nationwide discussion of segregation and discrimination, with even the National Guard walking children to their classes. Comic books were never more removed from reality than in the postwar era.

"Perception affects who will enter comics, as reader or creator."
SCOTT McCLOUD

Comics in the 1960s attempted to move toward a truer reflection of U.S. culture by introducing ethnic characters. Marvel Comics began to colorize pedestrians in street scenes and soon enough introduced two frontline black characters: Robbie Robertson, the parental editor-in-chief of the *Daily Bugle,* who had no superpowers but who played a key role in the life of Peter Parker (Spider-Man); and the Black Panther, a mysterious prince from an ambiguous African tribal nation who joined the Avengers as they were fighting a white-supremacist network. This minuscule investment of thought and ink went a long way toward convincing comics' still largely white reader base that ethnic diversity had been achieved.

Black characters abounded in the 1970s, but they tended to be heavy on race and light on individuality. The Black Panther was imitated in a number of characters loudly proclaiming their blackness, among them Black Lightning and Black Goliath. (For the record, Black Canary was not black—nor was she a canary.) Marvel Comics acknowledged this awkward stating of the obvious when the Thing joined forces with Black Goliath, sporting a newly designed costume, in an issue of *Marvel Two-in-One:*

> Why not complete the overhaul with a new name? I mean, it's pretty obvious that you're black, and if I remember my Sunday school lessons, Goliath was a bad guy.

Black Goliath changed his name right then to Giant-Man, a pedigree with a long, white history at Marvel.

Many black characters from the 1970s had stereotypical backstories involving ghettos and drugs (Falcon) or ambitions that were less noble than what readers had come to expect of heroes. Luke Cage, otherwise known as Power Man, rented himself out as a "hero for hire." He was later joined by Iron Fist, an absurdly dressed capitalization on the kung fu craze of the day.

Other ethnicities had less aggressive champions in the industry. Typically, one hero would embody the reputation of his or her ethnicity as a nod to diversity. Thunderhawk joined the new X-Men to represent Native Americans. Shang-Chi, master of kung fu, rode the wave of the 1970s fascination with martial arts.

The 1980s and 1990s served as correctives, killing off some ethnic characters, phasing out others and introducing more modest heroes. The roles of Green Lantern, Iron Man and even Superman were temporarily adopted by black men without demanding of them a representation of their entire race. A black woman became Captain Marvel—not "Black Marvel," or "She-Marvel," for that matter. And in the early twenty-first century, Captain America learned a startling truth: the super-soldier serum that gave him his enhanced strength and vitality was developed through failed experiments on African American soldiers. The face of American heroism had a history that included the exploitation of Black America.

"Open-minded white writers found it difficult to portray minority characters in a way that was not offensive or patronizing."
BRADFORD W. WRIGHT

The comic book industry over time has been coming to terms with its dubious history with ethnic characters, but the problem of marginalization has long been a concern of the genre. Comic books got their start during

Adolf Hitler's attempted genocide of European Jews, and the largely Jewish community of comics writers and artists did much to alert mainstream American culture to the moral problem and imminent threat of Nazism. Despite the wartime propagandizing that slanted American comics against the country's ethnic enemies, marginalization remained a running concern. With the creation of the X-Men, it became a defining theme of the industry.

X-MEN

Many of the early heroes in Marvel Comics were accidents of science—victims of radiation poisoning or applications of technology—or beneficiaries of mystical realities (Donald Blake found a walking stick that released Thor, the Norse god of thunder, into the world; Dr. Strange tapped into the world of magic and spirits). But the X-Men were born special, with powers that typically manifested themselves at adolescence. Charles Xavier started a school to train these young people in the use of their powers and to protect them from a bigoted, fearful public.

The "mutants" who made up this team were likable teenagers enduring much of the hardship common to the age group, but they faced the additional challenge of being forsaken, abandoned, mistrusted and even persecuted because of their genetic anomalies.

Many mutants couldn't hide their mutations if they wanted to. Some lack the maturity and the experience to control their powers: Rogue, for example, kissed a boy in the first *X-Men* movie, nearly killing him in the process by inadvertently absorbing all his kinetic energy. Others have mutations that involve changes to their physical appearance: Angel, for example, has wings, and Nightcrawler has blue skin and a tail.

Now, the frustration of not being able to control your body or the feeling that you look like a freak of nature are common adolescent concerns, but in the case of mutants those feelings are reinforced by the community in tangible and intangible ways. Derisive language and sputtering suspicion comes often to mutants on the streets, to the point where fearful mobs will hunt down a little child, as happened in the miniseries *Marvels*. Organized persecution has come in various forms, from the government enacting a Mutant Registration Act to a privately funded army of "sentinels" designed to flush out and neutralize mutants, and a national campaign of genocide.

Mutant reaction to such persecution has been mixed. Xavier works toward assimilation of mutants into the wider culture, promoting understanding and acceptance on one side, and ethical, responsible use of power on the other. Some groups, such as the Morlocks, withdraw altogether from mainstream society, developing their own culture underground. The third category, first organized and led by Magneto, sees mutants as a great leap forward on the evolutionary chain and sets itself in opposition to the non-mutant status quo, seeking liberation by any means necessary.

Xavier and Magneto have a long history together, dating back to young adulthood, that makes their parting of ways particularly tragic. Given the timing of their introduction to the comic book universe, they invite comparison to the competing racial visions of Martin Luther King Jr. and Malcolm X. But the storyline of the X-Men has been similarly embraced by gay readers as a parable of their experience. What is certain is that the X-Men have made it possible to see the human cost of marginalization in its various forms.

Marginalization has become a painfully clear problem in recent history. Adolescents, a key demographic for the comics industry, wrestle with in-crowd/out-crowd discrimination as a matter of course, in a sense as a side effect of growing into a personal identity. But some marginalization among high-schoolers in the late twentieth century has led to tragic ends, with students bringing guns to schools and giving violent vent to their feelings of isolation and rejection. More subtly, a culture that is in many ways obsessed with appearance and perfectibility leaves in its wake people who are painfully aware of their imperfections; some seek redemption through cosmetic surgery or obsessive exercise, others punish themselves for being imperfect through self-injury or other types of self-abuse, still others rage against the culture by disfiguring themselves with piercings or tattoos or even teeth-filings and tongue-forkings.

Similarly, people of non-Anglo ethnicity face an ongoing struggle against marginalization in a culture that ostensibly preaches full equal participation but in many aspects still segregates by default. Second-generation ethnic Americans, for example, face core identity crises: How Asian am I? Should I keep speaking Spanish at home? Does my neighbor think I'm a terrorist? Ethnic minorities struggle to find their identity as full participants in a majority culture that looks different from them while maintaining their identity as people of a particular background and culture.

Though people may be swept along by cultural tides and impersonal forces, they nevertheless remain distinct human beings with particular gifts to offer—gifts that often get overlooked as people pass judgment on their appearance, or even neglected as they cease to see themselves as being of any particular use. The task of the individual and the community is to find a level ground where diversity of all sorts, whether gender or age or ethnicity or personality, is given room to be, so that the strengths of individuals can be directed toward the common good. Thomas Merton recognized that the beginning of sainthood, a type of heroism we are each called to by our Creator, is a question of identity: "The problem of sanctity and salvation is in fact the problem of finding out who I am and of discovering my true self." That self, Merton knew well enough, does not exist in isolation, nor does the world begin to revolve around it once it's discovered. Frederick Buechner reveals the end of such sainthood in truly heroic language: "The place God calls you to is the place where your deep gladness [your secret identity] and the world's deep hunger meet."

Mutant heroes are often unwilling heroes, and they regularly face the temptation to hide their differences and let the world that flings such hatred and fear at them take care of itself, or to leave such a world altogether, or to use their special powers to get ahead either by force or by secret manipulation. The mutant Northstar, for example, used his exceptional speed to advance his competitive skiing career; Magneto left Earth to live by himself on an asteroid; Bobby Drake was asked by his mother, "Have you tried *not* being a mutant?"

In that sense, mutants are very much like women and ethnic minorities in the comic book industry, and indeed, in the broader culture. Women are in subtle ways encouraged to downplay their femininity to be taken more seriously by men in their careers, or to use their femininity to improve their standing in a competitive workplace. Sometimes they are taught to do both at the same time. Ethnic communities sometimes cloister themselves, reinforcing the idea that people who are alike only belong together, and people who are different belong apart.

The vision of the X-Men is similar to the vision of Martin Luther King Jr., calling for a common effort among diverse communities for a unified social purpose. Integration becomes a means to an end—employing the distinct contributions of the many for the greater good.

Integration by decree is a pivotal incremental step: although school desegregation, for example, did not solve the racial separation that characterized American culture of the 1950s, it forced previously separate and unequal communities to face each other and consider the question of racial justice. But though such considerations often begin at an institutional level, they are driven forward by a more theological impulse. The letter of the law may declare us equal regardless of gender or color or creed, but the spirit of any given law is equally circumvented or manipulated to serve our individualized interests. So despite our best efforts to integrate, the temptation to dis-integrate is always there. Some ultimately give in to these temptations, and though we can understand why, we mourn their decision. Others fight such temptations and embrace instead Xavier's vision of reconciliation. These we acknowledge as heroes, and on our best days we act like them.

X-CURSUS

Superheroes & Grownup Fanboys

*El Dragón used his mind to fix a **radio.** He used his mind to fix the box that gets voice and music from far away. It's easy for him to fix **radios.***

*Black Canary heard **music.** She heard the beautiful sounds of songs and tunes.*

THE SUPER DICTIONARY

*F*rank E. Lee is a DJ for WXRT Radio, a nationally honored station that has broadcast in Chicago for some thirty years, and he likes comic books. I heard him make a passing reference to DC's Elastic Lad, so I scurried home to visit the station's website and read his bio, which was filled with superhero references. Turns out his "fortress of solitude" is two suburbs over from mine, so I asked if we could get together. We talked about the influence of comic books on his view of the world and the challenges not only of being an adult fan of the medium but of being an arbiter of contemporary culture who has a habit that is perennially ridiculed.

"I have kind of a nerdy reputation with my coworkers, but they know I'm basically cool. I've always considered myself a type of superhero: 'Radio Man.' It's sort of a godlike power—you're all alone in the studio, and you say something, and people listen. And when you stop talking, some cool music or a heavily overproduced advertisement plays. You have great power; you could say something to cause a great havoc, if you wanted to. Of course, it would be the last thing you'd say on the air."

DJs are champions and victims of pop culture. Every word counts for a DJ, and their personalities are defined for their public by the music they play, the people they interview, the things that come off the top of their head. But a listening audience can be terribly fickle, and continuity can become a liability. To assert yourself as a fan of something that moves in and out of the cultural mainstream is risky—it reflects on your credibility as an expert on what is cool. The temptation to let someone else shape the culture is an industry-wide reality.

"Radio is tempted to play it safe. It used to be we'd play what we liked. Now it's all pre-programmed, demographically driven. It's either all old or all new. I think it's better, though, to look at things in context in order to get a full appreciation for the craft of what you're doing."

XRT has cultivated a reputation for crossing streams to consolidate the best of every era and genre of popular music—its DJs are scholars of popular music, in a sense. But that's not all they are. They have lives outside the studio they broadcast from. They may define what is best in contemporary music, but music does not ultimately define them. They are free to enjoy what they want. Lee is comfortable as himself: a parent, a music fan, a comics fan and a godlike Radio Man. Occasionally his worlds get to merge.

"I went on a ski trip for XRT, and a penciller for *The Legion of Super-Heroes* came along with us. He was happy to meet me, but I was a lot more happy to meet him. On the way back he drew Cosmic Boy, Saturn Girl and Lightning Lad and signed 'To Frank, a great every-now-and-then Legion reader. Long live the Legion! —Jeffrey Moi.' I go in and out of comic book collecting. It gets so expensive, and it's a little bit like a soap opera. You can get right back in, but you're going to miss a lot of plot development along the way."

A lot besides plot twists can happen along the way. Culture changes dramatically over time. Suburbs replace towns and cities; wars begin and end; political tensions rise and fall; social movements change an entire country's sense of civic duty. Things get written differently, but we also read things differently. "I'm a product of the modern science-fiction age. I was born in 1953, when we moved from the golden age into the silver age of comics. When I was

> *"It's considered normal in this society for children to combine words and pictures, so long as they grow out of it."*
>
> SCOTT McCLOUD

probably about ten years old, my uncle gave me a box of comic books some kids had left at his school. There were *Challengers of the Unknown*, a bunch of Marvel Comics, probably some other stuff. It was like being given a box of buried treasure.

"When I first started reading comics, it was an idealized world. The superheroes were really like gods in many ways. They had very few weaknesses, so the writers would try to come up with plots that would have some kind of challenge for the superheroes, and it got to be difficult after a while. So they'd invent weaknesses, or the hero's friends would get into all kinds of trouble. You never saw anybody die. I think it had to do with some kind of congressional oversight."

By the time Lee began reading comic books, the Comics Code was firmly in place, and the comics industry had long struggled to tell compelling stories without violating the rules established by the code to reinforce social order and stability. By the early 1960s, however, comics got their footing as Marvel looked at its characters from a different angle.

"Marvel made superheroes less godlike, more like real people, but savior types, like Jesus. Someone human but with great power, constantly tempted by things. It was still somewhat artificial at times. The characters were more fully fleshed out, but there still weren't deaths, no serious injuries. The general rule was, a comic book character isn't really dead until you see the body three times. You might see Superman in a coffin on a cover and you'd think, *Like they're going to kill off the golden goose!*

"New characters get around issues of age and dying, but you don't get the continuity. Old heroes, however, facing new challenges—I think that's very exciting. One of the reasons I named my daughter Kara is because she was born right after Supergirl died in *Crisis on Infinite Earths*. It kind of put an undue burden on her, I think. . . . Supergirl died, and for a long time she didn't come back. She's come back now, but she's not Kara—she's some other being."

That gets at the heart of superhero stories. They go on and on, and they depend, for the success of their industry, on issues that no one can emphatically claim to have mastered. Someone dies, and we think we understand what that means. Then she comes back, and we scratch our heads till we think we've made sense of that. But the field continues to confound us.

"I think there is an invisible, spirit world around us, but it's not something you can really perceive—you hope it's there, or maybe you're afraid it's there. Comic books put it right there in front of you. The best comics—like Alex Ross's *Marvels*—bring that fantastic reality to life.

"I used to wait for the new Justice League and X-Men like they were the word of God."

HOBART LINDSEY

"There are a lot of Superman references in songs lately. Dave Matthews Band has a couple of references in 'Where Are You Going,' and there are certainly others. I think the human condition is to look for someone who's going to be their savior. Superheroes are a fun way to look at that. They're like the ideal person, a modern god: someone who can right wrongs, someone noble, someone with the power to actually change things. I hate to use the word *escape,* but all fantastic literature gets at that. Plus they get the sense of wonder, the sense that the world is not just some cold, mechanical place."

And yet, the genre can never truly escape people's real-life experience. An alien invasion may be a temporary problem in a comic book, but an AIDS pandemic in Africa is a pervasive problem with no quick, foreseeable solution.

"Superheroes haven't been able to impose their will on the big questions. *Superman: Peace on Earth, Batman: War on Crime, Wonder Woman: Spirit of Truth* address issues like war or poverty, and the superheroes are helpless against them. Once Superman tried to prevent the death of President Kennedy, and it didn't work. I've heard it said that there's one thing superheroes can't do: come out of the paper. The Justice League has been strangely absent in the war on terror.

"But comics—and really all fantastic literature—give you a unique perspective on the world. They make you a little idealistic, make you think there is hope. Comics made me look at the world in black-and-white terms, good versus evil. They filter the real happenings of the outside world into the perspective of kids who read them. I think I had a better sense of how important things like the Cuban missile crisis were than my parents thought I did. We knew that nuclear weapons could annihilate *everybody,* and that opens the door to a lot of despair. But that kind of widespread devastation was what Superman faced every issue. I think comic books make you hope you can help to make the world a better place."

And perhaps that's what makes superheroes so attractive. They intervene into situations that seem to us beyond redemption, and they redeem them. They make us think that, with the right set of circumstances, we could help to fix the problems that might plague our world.

"Superheroes' greatest power tends to be that they're good people. The few times you see Superman turn bad you realize how horrible that can be. But then you're reminded that superheroes have an essential goodness to them. It inspires me to be a better person."

6

MY COUNTRY 'TIS OF THEE

Captain America & the Truth

*Hawkman gives his **allegiance** to his country. He says he will be true to his country and do all he can to help it.*

*This is a good **land**. This is a good country. Of all the **lands** in the world, I like this one most.*

THE SUPER DICTIONARY

Comic book superheroes were born and came of age in the bloodiest century of human history. American soldiers have read superhero comics in every military conflict since World War II. Superheroes have wrestled with the call to love of country and the duty to serve from their earliest days, and thanks to the human propensity for covetousness and conflict, they never get much chance to rest.

Patriotic superheroes of the 1930s and 1940s were victims of their own might: to enter Superman or Captain Marvel into the war with their extraordinary abilities would bring it to a premature end and make any following storyline preposterous. But to allow superheroes to be indifferent toward the war would clash with the widespread concept of heroism of the day, and to pretend that the war wasn't happening at all was equally absurd and would not satisfy the anxious reading population. So Superman failed his vision test (he inadvertently read a vision card from another room using his X-ray vision), and other heroes employed similar gimmicks to make them "unfit" to serve overseas and instead keep them available to cover the home front.

Meanwhile, new heroes were being cooked up to fight the Nazis, the Japanese and other foreign threats. Chief among them was Captain America, introduced months before the bombing of Pearl Harbor, which brought the United States into combat. The image on Captain America's inaugural cover showed him punching Adolf Hitler in the face, sending a double message to the comics audience: Hitler needed a good beating, and America was just the hero to give it.

> *"Comic books were really just contemporary fairy tales adapted to incorporate elements of current everyday life."*
> BRADFORD W. WRIGHT

Wartime comics quickly grew in popularity. They were read by troops and their loved ones on the home front as an idealized portrayal of the U.S. combat experience. Captain America was a scientifically enhanced version of any soldier: a little faster, a little stronger, a little greater endurance, perhaps, but driven by the same patriotic spirit that compelled the average G.I. The propaganda sold the very message that the idealistic reading audience wanted to buy—American soldiers were the best in the world, and each of them would submit himself to whatever the government could cook up to secure victory.

In 1945, war-bred superheroes were rendered obsolete by a new ultimate weapon, the atomic bomb. Its use in Hiroshima and Nagasaki decisively ended the war and the market for wartime comics. The war's comic heroes faded quickly; Captain America's comic was off the shelves by 1950.

Even homefront heroes suffered after World War II, as an older comics audience who had witnessed firsthand the terror of war and the horror of genocide grew tired of flashy heroes in brightly colored tights trading blows and puns with equally flashy villains. The next major American military conflict, on the Korean peninsula, generated war comics but no significant wartime superheroes. Bradford Wright sees the shift as a hint of the cultural malaise that would surface in the 1960s:

> The comic book market [of the 1950s] suggested that young people wanted more reality in their entertainment. They bought comic book versions of the world that indulged their anxieties, not ignored them.

Similarly, the growing political unrest on the exotic continent of Africa created a market for jungle comics, with female heroes notable not so much for their costumes as for their provocative lack of costume. The heyday of the superpowered, costumed hero had apparently passed.

REINVENTING THE ICON

More than a decade after his disappearance, Captain America was found floating in the Arctic Ocean, frozen in suspended animation. He was thawed out in 1963, just in time to define love of country for a generation of unrest and dissent.

The Captain America comics of the 1940s were comfortable making disparaging caricatures of the nationalities that made up America's enemies in World War II. Captain America's strategy was simple: beat down anyone who looked like a "Kraut" or a "Jap." But the Captain America of the 1960s fought on the home front, where an attitude of ethnic superiority marked the biggest cultural crisis of the day. Where should the symbol of America's greatness direct his energy when the only military action is an ambiguous presence in a tiny Asian country and the more pressing social concern is a looming civil war over civil rights?

Captain America stayed at home and wrestled with his own relevance.

The comic-buying audience of the sixties had not been of reading age during World War II, so reviving him was like creating a new character, with all kinds of angles to cover. Here was a man whose upbringing grouped him with the establishment and with parental culture—a Depression-era sensibility, a New Deal, wartime respect for government and a Humphrey Bogart/Superman sense of heroism—who was trapped in the body of a young adult, whose peers were restless, rebellious and energized by a sense of irony: heroes (such as Spider-Man, the Beatles, Martin Luther King Jr.) are a menace to society and a threat to the establishment, government inhibits social progress, war is arbitrary.

The largely unified war effort of the 1940s had been replaced by a stratified battle over an unpopular war in Vietnam. Captain America looked like the establishment—gung-ho law and order, fiercely anti-Communist and committed to the value and mission of the military—but comics appealed predominantly to a counterculture of young, activist skeptics who mistrusted the establishment, flirted with Communism and extra-American ideologies, and championed peace in defiance of the wartime culture around them.

So Captain America was out of his element, and he knew it. Writers used his character to speculate about the real virtues of American democracy, as he listened carefully to the new generation, embraced as allies some of Marvel Comics' first black superheroes (first the Black Panther, an expatriate from a country somewhere in revolutionary Africa, and later the drug-dealer-turned-hero Falcon), led a melting-pot team of Avengers from widely diverse backgrounds, and confronted domestic social challenges like racism rather than big, ideological dilemmas such as the containment of Communism.

He wasn't alone in this rediscovery of truth and justice. Comics could not ignore the reality of a new ethic, and to avoid being anachronistic and eventually disregarded altogether, each line of comics had to at least acknowledge the evolving understanding of the greater good. For DC

Comics, Green Lantern was led by Green Arrow into a fuller appreciation of the damage mainstream society had inadvertently wrought.
Green Arrow demanded that Green Lantern look beyond the letter of the
law to causes and effects, and gradually Green Lantern recognized that
some people stole because they could not get by in an economy that
abandoned whole neighborhoods when the promise of cheaper labor
beckoned it elsewhere, that some people used violence as a means of
equalizing systemic problems of discrimination, that some laws overlooked mitigating social factors and did not deserve to be enforced.
"Confronted with the sober realization that his Cold War assumptions
have been a lie," writes Bradford W. Wright, "Green Lantern begins to
understand that law and order [accidentals] are less important than truth
and justice [essentials]."

Superheroes were often misunderstood on the surface and confused
behind their masks during the 1960s—much like their writers and their
audience. But the 1960s only started the crisis of identity that would
come to a head in the 1970s and linger long into the future.

WATERGATE & A NATION OF NOMADS

Despite the high visibility of a liberal alternative direction for the country
and the ongoing frustration of a difficult, inexplicable war, Americans
voted twice to elect a law-and-order, staunchly anti-Communist, establishment president.

But events that took place during the Nixon administration crippled
the U.S. government in the eyes of its constituents. The *New York Times*
published papers from the Pentagon that revealed military secrets and
Vietnam War embarrassment. A flustered U.S. government fought to
keep the papers out of the news, but the public—and the courts—ex-
pressed little interest in protecting the secrets of the state. The state department had behaved just as a skeptical counterculture might expect,
and its credibility and authority were shaken.

More serious was the gradually unfolding story about illegal acts and dirty tricks undertaken by the president and his staff to keep and increase their power. President Nixon eventually resigned with a flourish of defiance, mild shame and feigned dignity. The figurehead of American democracy had failed to convince the world that he, and the government he led, was "not a crook."

A couple of years later, Nixon's successor pulled American troops out of Vietnam, leaving that country to carve out its own destiny. Soldiers returned home to an unsympathetic public even as draft-dodgers were invited to come out of exile with no questions asked. The nation now had an embarrassed military, an exposed state department, a disgraced former president and an exhausted public.

How would you like to walk around in a setting like that wearing an American flag on your chest? Disenchanted writers faced the challenge of writing stories for a disenchanted audience about a character who symbolized the object of their disenchantment.

And so, for a time, Captain America abandoned his own identity and became the Nomad. For ten years he had been carrying the burden of being a man out of time; now he was a man without a country. Eventually he returned to his traditional title and costume, but the disillusionment stuck, and Captain America's divorce from American government stuck.

So now, instead of representing America as a nation, our hero represented America as an idea. And his public would grow to count on that.

THE STRUGGLE FOR AMERICA'S SOUL

Since Watergate, patriotism has necessarily been redefined in the United States. Presidents are no longer above being subjected to criminal or ethics investigations; President Clinton even faced an impeachment proceeding.

At the same time, traditional patriotism ("My country, right or wrong") has occasionally driven popular opinion. Rambo and G.I. Joe were "real American heroes" as the struggle against global Communism came to a head during the 1980s. Country-western music in the aftermath of the terrorist attacks of 2001 shouted out America's greatness even as Canadian singer Celine Dion and the joint houses of the U.S. Congress belted out "God Bless America," and the president made a war on terror "the focus of my administration."

In the midst of this ambiguity about patriotism, two developments opened new frontiers for Captain America to explore. One took place in the pages of *The Avengers*. During a global crisis, the United Nations commissioned the superhero group, with Captain America as its head, to serve as a global peacekeeping force. This was a significant change for the Avengers, who previously had worked closely with the U.S. government. But perhaps more significant was the now global emphasis of the symbol of America. At a time when the real-world U.S. government was proclaiming the functional irrelevance of the United Nations, the comic book Captain America was linking his mission to the UN. Once again, the idea of America was found to be in tension with the real outworking of the American government.

Meanwhile, in a story arc called *Truth,* Captain America discovered that the super-soldier serum that had given him his power in 1941 had been perfected through experiments conducted on black soldiers. What had for sixty years been an example of American greatness now was exposed as an American atrocity. Captain America would be forced to reconcile these two truths: he had been empowered to fight against Hitler's Holocaust and champion racial equality in the face of militant supremacist groups, all thanks to the horrible exploitation of a racial minority.

And yet this development is part and parcel of the grander scheme of Captain America representing the idea of his country. Richard John Neuhaus refers to the United States as "the world's first creedal nation," exporting ideals such as all people being created equal and endowed by their Creator with certain, inalienable rights. But the drafters of the U.S.

Declaration of Independence also drafted the U.S. Constitution, which sanctions human property and grants three-fifths citizenship to slaves— a bold-faced declaration that all people are *not* created equal. The United States has expanded its territory by exploiting and abusing indigenous cultures; it has championed democracy throughout the world while occasionally propping up tyrannical dictators and violating basic human rights. The world's first creedal nation has a long track record of forsaking its creed.

Sadly, that is the nature of creeds. Like the United States, the Christian church, both as a community and as individuals, has an unfortunate record of bad behavior despite its central role in the shaping of modern morality. That's simply the way things go: people have good intentions but misguided actions, they generally behave themselves but occasionally do things they know they shouldn't, and they forsake their core commitments with surprising ease. We are products of our failures as much as of our ideals.

I came to terms with this duplicity in part by reading comic books. Captain America, as iconic as he is, is only one of many heroes who taught me as they learned that power does not lead inevitably to good, that any hero is one misstep from terror at all times, that one person's actions (or inaction) can be compounded into tragedy all too easily. My first visit to the Navajo reservation of northern Arizona forced me to deal with the fact that the richest country in the world—my country—contained people who lived in desperate poverty, and that I was doing nothing about it. I could, and I did, but I hadn't, and I regularly still don't.

Our ideals and our failures continue to live in tension with each other. We are not relieved of the responsibility to do justice and love mercy just because we recently did (or stopped doing) injustice and acted (or refused to act) mercilessly. Our call to be good and do right is constant, what we were created for. And we will surprise ourselves with our capacity for good if we do not allow our failures to finish us.

By virtue of being himself, Captain America had blood on his hands. And yet, by virtue of being himself, he had the capacity to do great and noble things for a world that desperately needed him. In this respect Captain America is not so special: with enough introspection each of us will see how we—as individuals, as arbitrary people groups and as citizens of sovereign nations—have the capacity to help and a heritage of wrongdoing to overcome. But it is this universality that makes Captain America so important: we are one with him, and he is one with us. His story, and ours, is not over.

MIGHT MAKES RIGHT

The Justice League Meets the Avengers

*Hurry, Hawkman. We **are** going to save the city. We **are** happy to help. We **are** the best people for the job.*

*Batman, Robin, Black Canary, and Green Arrow belong to a **club.** They belong to a group of people who are all interested in the same thing. . . . Catwoman chased Robin with a big **club.***

THE SUPER DICTIONARY

Superheroes congregate. It's a common occurrence in comic books. Groupings make good business sense—people who are interested in Spider-Man and Daredevil as individuals would likely pay to see them together. Groupings also make good aesthetic sense—to tell a story about someone with special powers fighting crime in a city where lots of people with special powers fight crime, you can avoid overlap for only so long.

But groupings can make good strategic sense too. A team can coordinate its movements, lend its collective support wherever a need might arise and count on one another to compensate for individual vulnerability. Hardly anyone can stop Batman now; what happens when he and the

Flash get together? Now add Superman and Aquaman to the mix, and suddenly a handful of people control the fate of the world. Ultimately, a team of the world's most powerful people has the potential to wield supreme power.

Beyond the sensibility of congregating is a clear human need for peer companionship. The last creative act in the opening chapters of the Bible, for example, is God's creation of a woman, for it was "not good that the man should be alone" (Genesis 2:18). Just so we're clear, this creation was not merely to fulfill the first man's sexual impulses; the first two humans are told by God to "fill the earth and subdue it" (Genesis 1:28). In a world full of people, being alone would no longer be a problem.

Except, of course, that being together can present its own problems. We each have an individualized consciousness and a social context, and the two rub up against each other. Meanwhile, we as individuals are growing and changing even as our context is changing. Where do I end and the world begin? Why must I submit myself to the rules of a family, organization, institution or culture when I disagree? At what point must I part ways, and when I reach that point, how do I then fill my need for association?

Superheroes who congregate face those nagging questions at an enhanced level. By themselves they are enviable—fighting successfully for truth and justice and whatever else might motivate them. But they are drawn together, and when they come together, often the impact is felt for generations.

THE AVENGERS

The Avengers were the first "super-group" in the Marvel Comics line. That is not to say that Marvel didn't already have teams of superheroes—after all, the Fantastic Four was Marvel's first great success in superhero comics. But the Avengers brought together strong-willed, larger than life heroes with independent fan bases. Every reader had a favorite: the cute couple Ant-Man and Wasp; the invincible Iron Man; the unpredictable Hulk; the conveniently rediscovered Captain America; or the literal god of thunder, Thor. The lineup quickly and regularly changed, but the title served its purpose: to showcase new Marvel talents and pool the assets of "Earth's mightiest heroes."

From early on the Avengers made ripples, serving as a launching pad for Marvel's first black hero, African prince Black Panther, and keeping the peace in New York and elsewhere while fighting organized networks of villains, alien

"The Avengers are there to ground me, to help me bring order into my life. They're good friends."
SCARLET WITCH

races and even a white supremacist group. The group was an institution, centering in a mansion complete with butler Jarvis, establishing a foundation to cover team expenses and fund stipends for unemployed team members, expanding to the West Coast, and linking their work to the U.S. government and eventually the United Nations through official liaisons. The Avengers weren't simply superheroes, they were high society. Any superhero who was anyone was a current or one-time member.

The Avengers turned heads over time as they took on various thorny issues. Their treatment of race was followed by uncharted ethical territory as android Vision fell in love with and ultimately married the mutant Scarlet Witch. Wonder Man discovered that he was a clone. Physically unusual heroes such as the Beast and Tigra won accolades while on duty but faced marginalization by the public when they went off the clock. Second-stringers faced layoffs by government decree. Founding member Henry Pym struggled to find his place first as Ant-Man, then as the original Giant-Man and eventually as Yellowjacket, all the while trying to undo the damage caused by his perfectly designed, artificially intelligent, amoral robot Ultron; he eventually suffered a nervous breakdown, beat his wife, betrayed his team and went to prison.

The Avengers wore their pettinesses on their sleeves, but for all the internal troubles they faced, the team—and the mansion that housed them—served as a safe retreat from the challenges of serving and protecting a fickle world that alternately trusted, revered, suspected and rejected their presence. The Avengers fought to keep a vulnerable world above water even as their leaders, in the words of the series' editors, fought to "instill as much trust in one another as the public has in the team itself. With the abundance of alpha personalities involved, and their diverse backgrounds, this is not an easy task."

THE JUSTICE LEAGUE OF AMERICA (JLA)

The Justice League was slower than the Avengers to complicate its original vision to tell stories of heroes together. The formula for the League was similar to that of the Avengers: An epic threat leads well-established superheroes to forge an alliance, and they stick together in case something too big for one of them comes along. Bad guys get beat, good guys banter back and forth, and the world gets saved. Pass Go, roll again.

The League was made up initially of DC Comics' greatest icons—Superman, Batman, Wonder Woman—and a strong supporting cast in the Flash, Green Lantern, Aquaman and the mysterious Martian Manhunter. The high familiarity of the principal players made the League a safe place to roll out newcomers and break into new audiences. *The Challenge of the Super Friends,* a Saturday morning cartoon featuring a distilled version of the League, won a strong fan base among Generation X and made otherwise undistinguished heroes such as Apache Chief and Black Lightning into doll-household names.

DC took a conservative approach to storytelling through JLA. Protecting the commodities of their brand leaders, and taking into account the young readership that came to the comics by way of the cartoon, "the original JLA tales . . . emphasized plot over characterization," according to Kurt Busiek. When market conditions proved safe for more sophisticated storytelling, with an aging fan base seeking out stories such as the postmodern superteam tale *The Watchmen* and the reinvention of JLA member Batman by writer Frank Miller, the League became a focal point for the maturing of the DC line. Eventually even the cartoons caught up to this maturation process. In 2001 a new *Justice League* cartoon was launched with a decidedly more serious tone: in the premier episode the team worked together to decimate an invading alien race, with no concern for keeping the aliens alive.

It should be said, however, that while DC approached risk to its principal players cautiously, by keeping readers at arm's length from them and portraying them in every circumstance as without self-doubt—as persistently "rational, mature, stable adults," in the words of Busiek—the company in the meantime told stories of nearly unimaginable scope. The bright world of DC comics faced wave upon wave of cosmic cataclysm, and if the regulars were already caught up in one wave, another set of heroes would rise to face the next. The League thus became a sort of rallying point for action, with new members starting out overwhelmed by the immensity of their teammates, and ending up overwhelmed by the immensity of the task facing the team. Some heroes stuck with it; others decided they couldn't cut it and stood down. Either way was OK for the League. It had limitless resources, the trust of an adoring Earth and a ready supply of new members, but the League also had the daunting responsibility of keeping a happy, peaceful world happy and peaceful.

So, the Avengers specialized in defense, we could say, and the Justice League specialized in offense. The League tried to make their world a better place; the Avengers tried to keep their world from falling apart. In a story thirty years in the making, those worlds collided, and in so doing, readers learned the role of power in shaping a world.

BATTLE OF TWO UNIVERSES

There's a long history of crossover activities between DC and Marvel Comics, but the mother of all crossovers kept eluding the two companies until 2003, when the right story and the right contributors lined up at the right time. The imminent destruction of two universes would bring together champions from each to fight for their future, and . . . well, so far, same old story. But what immediately comes to the fore in the *JLA/Avengers* four-issue team-up is the competing visions the teams have developed over time for what constitutes a good world.

Each team is temporarily transported to the other's world in search of twelve items that, taken together, can destroy either universe. The teams' initial scouting through their counterpart's world takes place in the first issue and makes immediate impressions on both teams. The Flash witnesses a mutant being chased by a hateful mob, which turns on him when he tries to intervene. Aquaman observes despot Dr. Doom exercising his harsh rule over the kingdom of Latveria and questions how a world could allow such tyranny to continue. The Martian Manhunter visits the devastated nation of Genosha, where genocide had been unleashed against mutants "for the crime of being different." Superman is the most shaken by what he observes. A self-designated guardian of Earth, he is shaken by "that world, that place. . . . If these were its heroes, I'm not impressed. Not with their world, not with their achievements. I'm not." Shortly thereafter he confronts the Avengers directly: "Your own world may be a sorry, disgraceful shambles—but you're not going to bring your madness to ours, as well!"

Superman isn't the only one who has cast judgment on the world he's visiting. As the Avengers enter the Justice League's universe, they're confronted with an unfamiliar reception: idolization. Onlookers swarm them for their autographs, a TV program broadcast from the side of a skyscraper shows off the reverence displayed toward the world's heroes, and Avenger Quicksilver, himself a regular victim of discrimination and persecution, learns of a museum devoted to the Flash and whole advertising campaigns exploiting the aura of superheroes. Captain America, having endured a lifetime of battling manipulators of cults of personality, sizes up the Justice League in a heartbeat: " 'Justice'—this isn't justice! . . . They must own this world, like little tin gods—demanding the public's adoration instead of protecting its freedoms! Don't you feel it? It's sour—it's wrong." When confronted by the Justice League, Captain America wastes little breath on them—"I knew you were fascist overlords"—before defining reality for his team: "If these high and mighty stormtroopers want to take us in, they'd better be prepared to take their lumps."

Gradually the teams realize that their mutual goals are better served by working together, but the die has been cast. In the eyes of the Justice League, the Avengers have let their world go to seed; they may be powerful, but they are not heroes. The best world is one where everyone is safe and secure, prosperous and at peace. The world of the Avengers cannot boast of such accomplishments, therefore the Avengers have failed in their mission.

In contrast, the Avengers determine that the heroes of the Justice League have abused their powers to shape their world in their own image, a world in which everyone is beautiful and no one hurts. The best world is one where human beings of whatever nature are allowed to be themselves and control their own destiny, within the boundaries of the individual. The world of the Avengers is allowed to remain diffuse, decentralized, in order to hold up that high value. The world of the Justice League has forsaken the individual in favor of an integrated system that is maintained essentially by its heroes. These heroes may be powerful, but they are not just.

THE WAY OF THE WORLDS

So, which is better—a world where people are free to direct their own destinies but where racism, despotism and random acts of carnage continue to hold their position, or a world where daily lives are lived in security and happiness but ultimate power is jealously guarded by heroes such as the Justice League or, worse, villains such as Lex Luthor? The Justice League approach reflects the sentiment of the World War II era its heroes sprang from: threats to the peace come from localized villains (Hitler, Stalin), and concentrated power is the most efficient means of preserving the peace (nuclear weapons, the United Nations). Bradford Wright observes, "In American society [of the 1930s-1940s] it took some might to make right after all." Under such a perspective, the world is a chessboard, with superpowers moving the pieces.

The Avengers' approach likewise reflects the worldview coming into focus at the time of its heroes' origins. The Avengers are a product of the 1960s, when young adults lost faith in the way their parents maintained the order of the world. The retreat to individual rights and personal freedoms that took place in the 1960s and the decades that followed are a consequence of that loss of faith. Good and evil battle in day to day events, and as observed by Aquaman in the crossover series, "Their world's stacked against them—so it seems like they've got to fight amazingly hard just to keep things on an even keel."

In a sense, the battle between these two worldviews fleshes out the inadequacies of each and ultimately presents the real problem to the rest of us. We are inheritors of the world shaped for a time by both of these worldviews, with all the benefits and consequences that they bring. We cannot be satisfied by the efforts of the Avengers, or the Vietnam generation, who are content to hold a disappointing world together. "As the culture of subsequent decades would demonstrate," writes Bradford Wright, "1960s activism could not compete very long with the narcissistic forces liberated at the same historical moment."

Nor can we be content with the place of force in the world of the Justice League, or the World War II generation. Jules Feiffer, a comics insider from the 1940s, sums up the problem generated by this approach:

"Once the odds were appraised honestly it was apparent you had to be super to get on in this world."

We are inheritors of both worldviews, and we may find it convenient to sit in judgment on the prevalent attitudes of these two generations, but we still have to live here, and to do so means we have to determine our own way. The advantage of having access to these templates is that we can learn from our forebears' mistakes and their successes. Despite concerns I might have about the ethics of power displayed in World War II—atomic weapons, totalitarian regimes, a lack of concern for civil liberties—the generation that introduced superheroes defeated Adolf Hitler and rebuilt Europe and Asia. Despite the moral confusion that came with the Vietnam generation that introduced the Avengers, we can thank them for great strides in racial and gender equality and care for the environment. We owe a lot to the people who came before us.

Besides, we judge generations and identify ourselves with our own generation because it's in our nature to congregate. We were designed for life together, and that means facing the difficult decisions that preceding generations have faced and recorded for us *as a community.* I benefit from the life experience of my parents and grandparents, but surely I also benefit from the insights of my peers. No matter what potential problems exist within communities, we still work best at fixing problems when we cooperate. And the chief lesson we can learn from the witness of the generations before us is that, in all likelihood, despite our greatest efforts and regardless of our ability to support one another in the task, we too will be inadequate to address all the trouble we will face. And at that point we'll have to decide where we can turn for help.

GODS WALK THE EARTH

Demigods, Daredevil & the
Problem of Religion

*No job is **impossible** for Supergirl. No job is too big or too hard for her to do.*

*Jonna Crisp went to **church** by rocket. She went to a place where people meet to think about God.*

THE SUPER DICTIONARY

Suppose you looked up in the sky and saw what appeared at first to be a bird, then a plane, then suddenly some kind of man. Then suppose that man landed effortlessly in front of you and offered to help you change the flat tire you had been cursing only moments before. And then suppose with one hand this man lifted your car above his head and, with a blast from his eyes, molded the rubber of the tire to fill in the hole and, with his mouth this time, blew the tire full of just the right amount of air. And then suppose he set the car down in its place, winked at you and flew off. How would you feel? Would you be embarrassed that you had been cursing? Would you be embarrassed that you had let such a mild inconvenience get to you so? Would you think you had seen an angel? a god?

In some comic books, you would have. There are many demigods and other immortal beings roaming the pages of a comic book universe, looking for a villain to vanquish or a mere mortal to serve. There are Greek gods, Norse gods, Daoist gods and Native American gods. Some of them even spend time together, commiserating about life with lesser beings and other godstuff. The polytheistic religions and ancient myths of the world have offered a lot of fuel for comic book storytelling, and really, why not? Here are beings reputed to have walked the earth on occasion, with powers beyond mortal ken, whose exploits have served to explain the inexplicable and inspire the unmotivated for centuries. What's the harm in making up some stories for them?

Largely absent from the comic book pantheon have been the representative gods of monotheistic religions. While a supreme-being, creator-type is hinted at by mystical characters such as the Spectre, by and large Allah and Jehovah are hard to find, nor have their prophets and apostles invaded the pages of mainstream superhero comic books. This too is understandable—no likeness of Jehovah is to be made (that's one of the Commandments); likewise, Allah is unrepresentable. And to interject their prophets into a comic story would not only offend their adherents but lead inevitably to an attempt to represent the unrepresentable. That's what prophets and apostles do—they direct people to their god.

Now, this is not to say that Allah and Jehovah have been absent from the comic book industry, but their association has been more, shall we say, mediated. Whereas some gods are unrepresentable, their religions are easily represented and in many cases are ideally suited to the comic book medium. Dorothy Sayers sees the words that make up Christian faith as a type of shorthand summarizing an experience driven by imagery: "The words of creeds come before our eyes and ears as pictures; we do not apprehend them as statements of experience." Graphic imagery has long been a staple in the telling of the Christian story, from the manger to the cross to the empty tomb, and further to the image of a fish symbolizing the fledgling movement. In the stations of the cross, the story of Christ's passion is presented in panel after panel of stained glass or other formats, and the experience is clearly evoked by the images in the mind of the observer. The paneled representation is a medieval Catholic accommodation to the largely illiterate culture of the Roman Empire; by passing through the stations a Catholic could experience the crucifixion of Jesus and learn orthodox Christian history. On the walls of every Catholic church, therefore, you can find a medieval type of comic book.

More so than in their presentation, comics by virtue of their subject matter make imaginable the idea that a god would come to earth to make his dwelling with his people, a central premise to Christianity. But the gods that make their presence known in superhero comics part from Christian orthodoxy in significant ways. Fundamentally, they come not to be worshiped or even to serve the human race; they serve a higher purpose: the purposes of the storyteller. Matthew Pustz acknowledges the ultimate end of this elevation: "In the Marvel Comics universe, . . . [creator Stan] Lee is even more important than God."

So, comic book gods may be heroic, but they are not necessarily godly. Seeing the limitations of a god among human beings in comic form won't tell us much about what the Creator of our own universe is like, but it may give us some insight into what he is not.

GREAT PRETENDERS

Hercules, a childhood hero of mine, is the product of conjugal union between Zeus, king of the Greek gods, and Alcmena, the wife of a Greek adventurer. Hercules became the strongest man alive and the subject of twelve great adventures. Marvel Comics brought him into its universe in the late 1960s.

Marvel characterizes Hercules as a fun-loving adventurer who quickly learns to love his new era. He enjoys a good fight, likes to celebrate his adventures over lots of alcohol and loves to woo the women around him. He is popular with his friends and teammates, often lightening a mood grown understandably tense over the imminent destruction of the universe, for example. He is a lovable cad, getting away with comments that other people would be legitimately sued or slapped for—"Don't mind him, he's just being Hercules." He is a prime example of what Bradford Wright identifies as a function of comic books: "a crude, exaggerated, and absurd caricature of the American experience tailored for young tastes." He is a god you would gladly hang out with but never think to worship.

In contrast to Hercules is Thor, Norse god of thunder who enters the Marvel universe by inhabiting the person of lame physician Donald Blake. At his origin Thor is occasionally summoned by Blake to right some wrong or serve some other heroic purpose, but over time Blake phases out of the storyline, his humanness subverted by Thor's divinity. He still walks the earth, but now always as a god.

Thor partners well with mere mortals, as a cofounder and nearly constant presence in the Avengers, according to Richard Reynolds:

> Thor enjoys battling alongside comrades such as Iron Man, Captain America and Hawkeye, even though he knows them to be vastly inferior to himself in raw power. He admires their heroism, and clearly enjoys his fellowship with them.

Nevertheless, Thor is a citizen of another realm, traveling regularly to Asgard to fulfill his obligations as son of the most high Odin. Thor is characteristically aloof, aware of his divinity and occasionally incensed by humanity.

Thor has a loyal fan base, reverential even, and defensive of his divinity. Indeed, in his book *Get the Word Out* John Teter tells of a college student who, when asked to pray, addressed his prayer to Thor's father,

Odin. But Thor's story does not fit neatly in the affairs of mere mortals. He is confused by human behavior much of the time and always clear about his separation from them. Hercules lives beneath the dignity of a god by indulging himself in human entertainment, but at least you can talk to him.

Thor and Hercules actually get along quite well, all things considered. Each is a provincial god removed from his province, and though Norse mythology and Greek mythology have no historic connection, their common experience as gods out of time and place presents them with common problems that they help each other through—a sort of divine support group.

UNGODLY GODS

The matter-of-fact acceptance of historic gods among normal (or, let's face it, supernormal) human beings is both a consequence of comic book storytelling and a statement about religious pluralism in a global community. These gods have not been revered as orthodox by any culture in thousands of years, yet their divinity is a critical aspect of their character. The reader must entertain the notion that higher powers exist and interact with this world. The gods in play, however, make no claims of having created this reality or of exercising utter sovereignty over it. Thor, for example, never wins a battle by speaking his enemies out of existence. He hits them, hard and frequently, but he never de-creates them. Nor do the comic book gods make any attempt to dictate morality. Even if they wanted to, they would not be allowed in any real sense, as Bradford Wright notes:

> As Marvel insisted, anyone who moved through society disguising their intolerance as morality was a far greater menace than the nonconformists whom he persecuted.

Each comic book universe is stocked so full of gods and their human counterparts that divinity seems insignificant. The casual observer, and by association the reader, are led to conclude that gods are a dime a dozen, nothing special. Indeed, there are nongods who exercise more godlike power than their divine counterparts.

Marvel's Watcher, from a universal race of Watchers, observes every event that takes place on the earth and interprets it for the archives of creation, even tracing the history of counterfactuals, the effects of causes that never happened. *What If . . .* comics told stories such as "What if Wolverine had killed the Hulk" which further developed characters for the reader without intruding on the one true storyline. The Watchers' code of conduct pledges noninterference in the actual development of each world, so although our Watcher has a great fondness for the people of Earth, he will never intervene to deliver us from evil.

No, in a comic book universe, gods must make a decision: they will behave as gods and forsake meaningful interaction with humanity, or they will engage humanity to some degree and, to that degree, cease to be gods in any meaningful sense. Ultimately, a chasm exists between God and humanity. The Watcher chooses essentially to live on the divine side; Hercules chooses the human side. Thor may fly from one side to the other on occasion, but the chasm is still present and never finally bridged. Mere mortals play hosts to these gods but not as citizens of their kingdom or as subjects of their regency. There are gods, and there are humans, and only occasionally do they get together.

Thus, religion in comic books is necessarily less about divine-human encounters and more about a search for meaning.

SON OF NUN

Irish Catholic Matt Murdock was born in Hell's Kitchen, New York. He didn't meet his mother till years later when she nursed him back to health after a systematic campaign to destroy his life. Instead, he was raised by his father, a prizefighter who eventually was murdered when he ran afoul of the crime syndicate that controlled his fights. An accident in his childhood left Matt blind but intensified his remaining senses and gave him a kind of radar, which he honed into a skill under the tutelage of a mystical martial arts master named Stick. His skills and training ultimately would help him to fight crime by night, even as he practiced law by day. He took the name Daredevil in honor of his father, who "fought like the devil."

We come to learn with Matt that his mother was a nun in Hell's Kitchen, that she knew about his special talents and had been watching him all along. She was there for him on occasions when he felt incapacitated by his blindness, when he struggled to maintain his sanity and when his experiences of human depravity drove him to resent God. Matt's mother, the sister, became a kind of godmother to a devil in Hell's Kitchen.

Daredevil stories bridge a gulf between the supernatural and the everyday. We're exposed to organized crime, drugs, prostitution, petty crime, gangland violence and political corruption—all the hallmarks of a city in trouble. And we don't witness them from far off. Matt may be our hero, but we love to see him suffer. In the words of Richard Reynolds, "Heroes need to triumph in the short term, but they can never be said to live happily ever after." Matt loses people close to him on a regular basis by radically diverse means, from assassinations to personal betrayals to mental illness to AIDS to a simple drifting apart. We see him close to losing it often, tempted to give in to revenge, to madness, to despair. In Daredevil stories we see the everyday realities of pain and hardship challenging the weak and the strong, the individual and the community.

"In a medium associated with escapism, any concession to the real world may be striking. 'We must find the orb of power or all mankind is doomed!' 'Yes! But first—to the men's room!'"

SCOTT McCLOUD

But Daredevil stories take us

to the other side of reality as well. Writer Frank Miller made Matt a witness to the resurrection of his lover Elektra. Anne Nocenti took Daredevil through a literal hell and out the other side. Kevin Smith dropped him into a tale of the apocalypse—our hero found himself running interference for the second coming of Christ. The film *Daredevil* gave Matt opportunities to consider his vocation as a vigilante during his confessional time with a priest, and a climactic battle took place within the walls of the church. Daredevil action figures are sold with a stained glass backdrop—a window that lets a blind man see the spiritual breaking into the everyday.

IN VIEW OF THE ULTIMATE

If you were a superhero, how could you get through a day without wondering about the origin of reality, without questioning how you came to be so specially gifted? If you were a superhero, how could you avoid demanding an accounting from God for the pain and suffering you witness day in and day out, even the evil you know is taking place while you're otherwise occupied? In light of the things you would have witnessed, the experiences you would have had, the undeniable wonder of your own creation, you would have to work awfully hard to avoid raising such questions.

In a sense, the comic book industry has been an attempt to offer an explanation for all those questions. We feel special; perhaps it's because there's something so unique about us that only we can prevent a particular type of evil from manifesting itself in the world. We witness or experience pain and suffering; perhaps it's because some nefarious villain is making a play for power that ultimately someone with an inordinate amount of willpower and giftedness will confront—as in the experience of the dangerous Dr. Vreekill at the 1940 New York World's Fair, whose monomaniacal rant was interrupted as Batman and Robin came crashing through the window: "Power shall be mine! I shall be king of crime! I—

huh?" We hear about tragedy taking place outside our immediate experience, and we wonder why nobody has risen up to address the problems of a troubled world.

Ultimately, the search for meaning in a comic book story becomes irrevocably disconnected from the reader's own search for meaning. The reader may reasonably expect to experience some amount of suffering, to witness some degree of evil, to feel some stirring of the heart to act. The reader may be exposed to gods-on-paper who come across as human or as divinely aloof as the storyteller dictates. But matters of spirituality in stories of superheroes never quite break out of their two dimensions. The reader needs a god big enough to face the very real, very three-dimensional evil in and among all of us.

EVIL IS AS EVIL DOES

Lex Luthor, Magneto & Galactus

*The Penguin is a **bad** man. He is not good. He is **worse** when he plays tricks. He is **worst** when he is mean.*

*Oh! Someone is making **trouble** for Flash. Someone is making a hard time for him. Why does he have such **troubles?***

*Lex Luthor needs a **lesson** in being good. He needs to be taught how to be good. In fact, he needs many **lessons.***

THE SUPER DICTIONARY

Evil used to be so straightforward. Evil people used to identify themselves as such, making it easy for a superhero to tell who needed rescuing and who needed jail time. Back in the day, villains had clear objectives—break into Fort Knox, steal the crown jewels, subject Batman and Robin to a slow, torturous death—and well-marked tools to do the job, such as giant magnifying glasses to focus the sun's heat on the Dynamic Duo's simmering brains. Villains allied themselves with other villains and gave themselves group names like the Sinister Six, the Masters of Evil or the Legion of Doom. They were clearly the antithesis of everything our heroes were about.

These days, however, evil has become nebulous, and villains have become sympathetic. Tales abound of college ethics classes who cannot conclude with confidence that, among other things, Nazi Germany committed evil by attempting to eradicate the Jews. The television series *Angel* featured heroic vampires who only occasionally become homicidal, and *Alias* lulls us into trusting characters who we ultimately learn are traitors and double agents. *The Sopranos* told the story of working-class hero Tony Soprano, a mob boss seeking professional counseling. Classically evil behavior—murder, thievery, mayhem and so on—has been successfully presented in ways that make it difficult to categorically condemn such acts *as* evil behavior. There's no doubt about it: evil isn't as simple as it used to be.

Author Walt Wangerin points out that the quintessential evil act—the selling of Jesus by Judas Iscariot—was recorded with no insight into Judas's rationale. Theories range from simple greed (Judas was paid thirty pieces of silver to betray Jesus to the Sanhedrin) to disillusioned revenge (Judas was a zealot who resented Jesus' pacifist posture toward the imperial government), but no final explanation is offered in Scripture. Wangerin suggests that this is the case because evil at its core has no justification: evil simply is, and to waste time trying to understand it is to waste precious energy that would be better devoted to overcoming it and guarding against it.

Yet even such seemingly straightforward tasks as overcoming or guarding against evil become murky prospects when you consider how difficult it is to define it. One person's evil offense is often another person's righteous act. What was so comical about teams like the Masters of Evil (or the later New Masters of Evil) was that they didn't mind calling themselves evil. They lacked a subtlety that the evil we experience in reality would never lack. Evil is perplexing because it is intentionally subdued—such that the patron saint of evil, Satan, disguises himself as an angel of light (2 Corinthians 11:14). It is confusing because it is often practiced with good intentions; victims of terror attacks would be horrified to hear perpetrators celebrating their actions, but that doesn't stop the celebration. More unsettling still, as with the brothers of Jewish patriarch Joseph, malicious evil sometimes brings about good (Genesis 50:20).

What is evil, and what causes it? These questions plague every conscience at one time or another. It's a very present question to comic book superheroes, because it's what keeps them in business. It's also what keeps comic book companies in business, and as such, the writers and artists behind comic books have gotten very good at imagining all kinds of opponents for their heroes—even the kind that makes you cheer, even the kind that makes you wonder.

THE SINNER: LEX LUTHOR

Lex Luthor's name is almost as recognizable as Lois Lane's or Clark Kent's. Luthor is a principal character in the first two *Superman* films and in the *Smallville* television series; he was a founding member of the Legion of Doom on television's *Super Friends;* and he has a fifty-plus year career in comic books. He is the quintessential villain in comic books, the arch-nemesis in Superman's long list of enemies. His ambition is matched only by his accomplishments, and his villainy is equaled only by his sophistication.

"Have you ever wanted to make a great evil plan but didn't have the time or superhuman intelligence? You're not alone. . . . The secret to success is planning ahead."

HOW TO BE A VILLAIN

If Superman is the definitive good, Lex Luthor is the definitive evil. Motivated, apparently, entirely by self-interest, he has built himself a material empire by outwitting and usurping anyone who gets in his way. He has a knack for turning adversity into opportunity, even turning the sale of his soul to the devil to his own advantage. In *Superman: The Man of Tomorrow* #3, a deal with the devil turns temporarily sour, and Luthor finds himself trapped in a snow globe in hell, until a space-time rift drops him just outside of Las Vegas. Luthor dismisses his Faustian bargain as he plans his next move.

> The very idea of a living devil is as absurd as the existence of the soul! . . . Surely I'd have felt some sort of loss if I'd really given up a "soul." . . . Besides, if there really was anything to this soul nonsense—I'd have lost mine long ago.

Luthor sets himself against "the alien" Superman as two equal, opposing forces. Luthor, convinced that his successes in life prove his worldview correct, is stymied by Superman's great power and apparent altruism. Since they inhabit the same city, their paths often cross. Superman's agenda is straightforward—truth and justice—but Luthor's vendetta against him is nuanced by his obsession with power. Given the right set of circumstances, Luthor will go the extra mile to help Superman out.

> The solution to the alien's dilemma could be solved . . . easily. As always, the question is this: do I gain more from Superman's suffering—or his salvation?

Luthor's origin story changes from medium to medium. *Smallville* presents him as a morally complex child of great wealth, estranged from his devious and manipulative father and desperate to assert his distinct identity. The show takes viewers through a prolonged, subtle and ultimately tragic descent into the adult Luthor known by the audience to be Superman's enemy. The 1989 *Lex Luthor: The Unauthorized Biography*, by contrast, portrays Luthor as a self-made man, a child of loser parents, who exploits every opportunity to advance himself. He ultimately presents his agenda to his biographer before having him killed:

> Life is short. . . . I chose to become a god. I control human lives,

instead of being controlled. . . . Which is why I cannot abide Superman! There is only room for one god on this planet! I'm determined to bring him down at all cost!

There you have it: a battle for the world fought by two supreme beings. A dualist worldview casts evil in this framework, but it's also a common presumption from antiquity. The psalmist acknowledged as much: "Bad guys have it in for the good guys—obsessed with doing them in" (Psalm 37:12 *The Message*). The film *Unbreakable* embraces this theme, as the exceptionally fragile "Mr. Glass" goes to great lengths to uncover his superhuman opposite. He can barely contain his exuberance as he ultimately shares the whole story of how he discovered the connection between him and the story's hero—they are two parts of one whole.

> *"One thing you can always count on a villain to do is explain his plan. There's this thing about bad guys, like they never got enough attention as kids."*
> SPEEDY, FASTEST SIDEKICK ALIVE

A self-contained equilibrium of good versus evil brings some comfort to some people. The idea that good and evil can be easily categorized and dismissed as a natural state can give people a sense of stoic contentedness, a sense that everything is as it should be, no matter how bad it gets. If good and evil are equally matched, we don't have to think about either one. But the problem is that good and evil rarely seem evenly matched. What's more, what is perceived as evil by one person might easily be perceived as good by another, as readers experience in the story of Magneto.

THE ZEALOT: MAGNETO

Magneto from the beginning has been a different kind of villain from Lex Luthor and his ilk. The perfect foil for the X-Men's Professor X, Magneto is a mutant with the ability to control magnetic fields. He sees his power, and the powers bestowed on other mutants, as evidence that the evolutionary chain is expanding, leaving humankind (Homo sapiens) behind, as mutants (Homo superior) claim their destiny as the dominant species.

Magneto was introduced to the world as a villain, early in the X-Men's history designating himself leader of the Brotherhood of Evil Mutants. Magneto was the sworn enemy of nonmutant humans, the latest in a string of misanthropes that included the brutish Hulk and, dating back to the 1940s, the prince of Atlantis, Namor the Sub-Mariner.

Over time we learned that being misanthropic didn't necessarily make one evil. Namor set aside his differences with "surface dwellers" to fight alongside Captain America against the Nazis in World War II. As indignant and dangerous as the Hulk is, he has always been essentially good and a sympathetic character for his audience. And so by the time Magneto entered the Marvel universe, the ground had already been laid: evil is in the eyes of the beholder.

Magneto sees the struggle for dominance as a game of survival of the fittest. Though his official position is that mutantkind is the evolutionary superior to humankind—and thus humans are living on borrowed time, to be disposed of when they become too troublesome—in reality he thinks defensively. Magneto has firsthand experience of human evil, having suffered abuse, alienation and even governmental persecution because he was different. The series of films based on X-Men comics portrays Magneto as a survivor of the Nazi Holocaust and shows him beaten mercilessly by a prison guard. The relaunched comic book series *X-Men* #1 (1991) has Magneto living alone on an asteroid until a group of mutants convinces him to reignite a mutant-human cold war by reminding him of a campaign of genocide one nation had waged against mutants. Considering all Magneto has experienced, it's often hard to remember that he's the bad guy.

In fact, Magneto has frequently played the good guy, temporarily embracing a vision of peace between mutants and humans, even temporarily leading the X-Men on behalf of the more idealistic Professor X. He is, at the heart, a zealot driven by principles to act.

But zealotry, no matter how well intended, is dangerous. Zealots have murdered doctors for performing abortions; zealots have blown up buildings to promote their political agendas. But zealots are often victims rather than perpetrators of violence: Jesus warned his followers of the cost of discipleship by reminding them that defenders of the status quo often kill countercultural prophets (Matthew 23:37; John 16:2-3). Zealotry often serves a cause well, rousing people to action and getting things done. But zealotry generally also gives evidence to just how difficult evil can be to precisely identify or avoid. In some cases, we may be fighting what we think is evil only to find that we're actually perpetrating evil against the ultimate good (Acts 5:33-39) or kicking the goads of an unstoppable force (Acts 9:5).

THE UNSTOPPABLE FORCE: GALACTUS

Galactus is not your everyday villain. John Byrne tells the story of the character's creation in an introduction to *Fantastic Four: The Trial of Galactus*.

> In 1966 Stan Lee and Jack Kirby created a character like none who had ever appeared before in the annals of comic book fantasy. . . .
>
> Legend has it that Stan's instructions to Jack . . . were astonishingly simple and to the point. Supposedly he sent Jack a "plot" which consisted of nothing more or less than four words: "Have them fight God."

God as a villain? You would hardly think it possible, but Kirby and Lee crafted a character who could be described as little less. Galactus came to Earth to destroy it—not as part of some nefarious plot to seize power from someone else, not out of revenge for some earthly wrong done to him, but simply because he literally eats planets for breakfast.

Galactus, we come to know, is spoken of throughout the universe as the Devourer (or Ravager) of Worlds. A herald precedes him to prepare each world to be consumed, but in the series titled *Marvels* by Kurt Busiek and Alex Ross, Galactus announces his own intent: "My journey has ended! This planet shall sustain me until it has been drained of all elemental life! So speaks Galactus!" Other characters in the story refer to the event as "judgment day" or "apocalypse," but the final revelation comes from Galactus and no other.

Galactus ultimately relents from his plan to eat the earth. He is not defeated by the Fantastic Four so much as "stymied" by them, and he decides that the earth should live on. But that does not prevent him from continuing to devour worlds. Such is the way of Galactus, and no other world seems capable of stopping him. *The Trial of Galactus* gives the reader insight into who Galactus is to the universe, and who he is to himself.

> I am power which is beyond power, knowledge which is beyond thought! . . . You are but a fading shadow of my cosmic all! . . .
>
> Am I not Galactus? Am I not he whose very name is spoken only in dread whispers throughout the farthest reaches of the unending universe?

Galactus's origin predates the creation of this universe, but he does indeed have an origin, which means he is a created being, despite his reputation as a god. After an act of kindness from the Fantastic Four that saves his life, Galactus wrestles with the morality of his world-consuming until he is visited by Death, whose origins and purposes are intimately associated with his. Death hints at what we will soon be told explicitly:

> You and I are as old as creation, sibling, yet we are but children, mere babes not yet to know maturity until that distant time when the cosmos shall achieve its final end. And the nature of that end is set and written, Galactus. You and I are but the shepherds who

guide it to its proper purpose. Or more precisely, it is a tangled garden you and I must ever weed. . . . Yours is quite possibly the most important role. Do not shirk it, lest the universe fail at the last.

Galactus goes on to consume the throne world of the Skrulls, a despicable alien species who have plagued the earth and the universe with war-mongering and imperialism, but seven billion souls nonetheless. Reed Richards, leader of the Fantastic Four and inventor of the device that restored Galactus to life, is brought to trial at an intergalactic court. Since the god Galactus cannot be held to account for his actions, the universe will condemn those who aid and abet him instead.

Reed is, of course, guilty of saving Galactus's life, and so he has little to offer in his defense. But the trial of Reed Richards is really the trial of Galactus, and Galactus, it turns out, has many defenders with unimpeachable credentials. First witness: the Watcher, one of a race of beings who chronicle the events of universal history. He testifies that "there is about Galactus much more than mere mortal minds can ever comprehend. . . . Do not doubt that Galactus has a purpose. There is an order of things in this universe. One such as he would not be permitted to exist unless he had a place in it."

Reed speaks in his own defense along a similar line:

We were told by the Watcher that [Galactus] was not evil—that Galactus is in fact beyond good and evil. . . . If a being is truly neither good nor evil he is by definition neutral. Yet clearly Galactus is not a neutral being. . . . His effect is catastrophic to say the least. . . .

Albert Einstein once said that "God does not play at dice." He meant that there is an order of things in our universe. And it does not require belief in a supreme being to realize that Galactus must somehow be part of that order. . . . For if he is truly to be considered neutral, then the apparent evil of his actions, must, in the end result, not be evil. And so, they must be part of some greater good.

Reed's self-defense is not compelling for all sorts of reasons. He relies "on logic and faith," but his logic is strained. He presumes that Galactus is neutral; that neutrality is not evil but instead by perpetrating evil contributes ultimately to good. Follow that logic if you can; theologian Henri Blocher "shudders at the thought of this [type of] complete indulgence." The death of seven billion beings cannot be fathomed as a good thing; "spontaneously and wholeheartedly we say 'No!' to it."

Indeed, Reed's accuser dismisses his claims as "a child's game of arithmetic." But more witnesses step to his defense, including Odin, the god of Norse mythology and as such one of those supreme beings Reed is not required to believe in. Odin tells the tale of Galactus's origin, which dates to the origin of the universe:

> That fateful day . . . Galactus lived! Thus was born into the new universe a new natural force. Like the solar wind, like the supernova. . . . To each world in time he comes and his very coming is a test. Those that pass the test are strengthened by it, and made more worthy of that great fate which is the promised end of our universe. Those that fail, fail totally and are forever expunged, wiped from the slate of time and space.

Pretty heady stuff, but the jurors remain unconvinced until the final witness stitches it all together. Eternity—not so much a god as a universal mind—is summoned and joins all minds present together, until they all sense that Galactus is, just as they are; he belongs, just as they do; and he, as they, serves the purposes of eternity. In *The Trial of Galactus,* as in many solutions to the problem of evil, "evil becomes a kind of auxiliary motor . . . to prevent us from getting stuck at the present stage of Evolution." Galactus offers an optimistic sort of evil, in the language of Blocher—the type of evil we can celebrate as a catalyst for the long-term good of all creation.

EVERYDAY EVIL AND THE WAY OUT

So are we supposed to just grin and bear the cosmic forces that bring evil to bear on us? Are we all inescapably set in mortal conflict with our opposites, as Superman is with Lex Luthor? Are we doomed to seek blindly the good as we understand it while justifying whatever evil we commit along the way, as in the case of Magneto? Is there any satisfactory, discernible logic to evil?

Blocher offers the remedial definition of evil as anything "that occurs in experience and ought not to." That's really all we need to know about evil, isn't it? "For a humanity that is overwhelmed by suffering (evil endured) and guilt (evil committed), . . . [How long?] is the question that matters."

In our everyday experience we are probably less like the nefarious Lex Luthor or the purpose-driven zealot Magneto or the force of nature Galactus—we are even less like Reed Richards or Professor X or Superman—and more like Batman's former friend and district attorney Harvey Dent, who finds himself torn in two when a criminal disfigures one side of his face. Harvey takes the name Two-Face and begins deciding whether he will do good or evil deeds based on the flip of a coin. No one—from Batman to the people of Gotham to the readers, even Harvey himself—knows from one minute to the next whether his next move will cause harm or serve the cause of redemption. He is at once a villain and a tragic hero, the victim of circumstance who can't find his way out of a cycle of confusion.

If the idea that we have so much in common with a disfigured, deranged sociopath is too uncomfortable, consider that we are also quite a lot like Hal Jordan, who for a time served as Earth's cosmic defender, Green Lantern, and wielded one of the most powerful tools in the universe. Hal had good intentions, but in his desire to resurrect his city and the people he loved, he made a series of well-intended mistakes that nearly destroyed the universe. Hal determined that the source of his power ring was capable of reconstructing reality to bring his ruined city back to life, but the stewards of that power source were unwilling to give him access to it. The ensuing power struggle saw Hal kill close friends and threaten the universe's equilibrium—all with the aim of doing what he thought was the right thing.

Hmm. Perhaps our own agendas are not as unequivocally good as we think. Do we really know from one moment to the next whether we will abuse what power we have (and we do have power, no matter how proudly we declare ourselves the underdog) or whether our decisions are leading us down a redemptive path? Do we really control our power as effectively as we think? Adam and Eve sought to harness the knowledge of good and evil, and ultimately unleashed the human capacity to cause devastation on a daily basis. When we're honest, we recognize that we, as individuals and as a species, lack the capacity to master good and evil. The question for all and for each of us is as urgent as it is pragmatic: Who will save us—who will save me—from this body of death (Romans 7:24)?

HOLY CASE STUDY!

Superman Versus Jesus

*Superman came to **save** us.*

*I am the friend of all **people.** I am the friend of all men, women, girls and boys.*

THE SUPER DICTIONARY

The first night of my freshman year at college, after my parents unceremoniously dumped me at my dorm, my new roommate—a junior religion major and a chain pot-smoker—lit up a bong, took a hit and asked me what I thought of Jesus. I was a bit dumbstruck by the events taking place, and I had no firm opinion of Jesus at the time, so I winged it. Jesus, I decided, was the superhero of his era, invested with powers no one else had and exercising those powers for the good of all humankind. My new roommate had apparently moved on, because that ended our discussion.

But my hastily drawn conclusion opened up new questions for me. If Jesus had all these powers, why did the people kill him? Why didn't he fight his way free? How could he allow such evil to take place? And if Jesus were not a superhero but rather God, I had the same questions.

HE CAME TO SET THE CAPTIVES FREE

Superman, like all Western hero myths, cannot ignore the story of Jesus. Jesus represents, among other things, what we expect to need and don't believe we ourselves can provide. He serves as the ultimate role model for what is heroic and noble and even superhuman. If there weren't traces of Jesus in Western myths, we would have created them. Robert Farrar Capon highlights this borrowing:

> "Faster than a speeding bullet, more powerful than a locomotive, able to leap tall buildings in a single bound. It's Superman! Strange visitor from another planet, who came to earth with powers and abilities far beyond those of mortal men, and who, disguised as Clark Kent, mild-mannered reporter for a great metropolitan newspaper, fights a never-ending battle for truth, justice and the American Way." If that isn't popular christology, I'll eat my hat.

We can attribute this plundering of Jesus in part to the ethical system he laid down. Jesus established a code of belief and behavior more durable than any that preceded it, one crafted and immediately tested in an atmosphere of powerlessness. When Jesus told his listeners to go the extra mile and turn the other cheek, he was talking to citizens of an occupied territory, ruled by imperialist thugs, not to comfortable, autonomous suburbanites in a free-market democracy. Jesus defined the good by the act itself, not by the consequences of the act.

But Jesus brought more than an ethical code. He drew people's attention to the intentions of the heart in an era of hypocrisy and showmanship. Those who did things to gain favor with God were essentially similar to those who acted to gain favor with the Romans, the religious hierarchy or the common people. The good was defined by its purity and authenticity—the good was self-evident.

So Jesus made simple what centuries of bureaucracy and politics had made complex: love God, love your neighbor. But what further distinguished Jesus from those authors of ethical codes before and since him—what forever sets him apart—were his actions that defied logic and physics and decorum. Jesus completed the concept of heroism through his purely benevolent use of his unfathomable power. Western heroes to follow Jesus would never escape his shadow. Superman would be no different.

AMERICAN WAY, TRUTH, LIFE

Fast-forward nineteen hundred years. Albert Schweitzer had sought to determine the historical reliability of Jesus' story, as told in the Bible, and inadvertently brought Jesus' divinity into question; Sigmund Freud had sanctified self-interest; and Friedrich Nietzsche had put forth the Superman hypothesis—that some people are born to control the destinies of others.

"Twentieth-century America demanded a superhero who would resolve the tensions of individuals in an increasingly urban, consumer-driven, and anonymous mass society."
BRADFORD W. WRIGHT

The United States came of age as these ideas were being established and disseminated, and it found its place on the world stage as charismatic presidents such as Theodore Roosevelt, Woodrow Wilson and Franklin Roosevelt took leadership roles in resolving international dilemmas. Trendy ideas such as social Darwinism (the best suited to a culture or economy become dominant) and the undeniable strength of the nation evidenced in the First World War combined to renew America's self-understanding as a city on a hill, uniquely qualified to direct the course of human events. The first superhero with mass appeal set up shop in America and took his name from Nietzsche's theories.

In the beginning, Superman made his dwelling among everyday people. He fought villains who corrupted such otherwise pure ideals as truth, justice and the American way: democracy, capitalism and scientific advancement. Dirty cops, profiteering corporate executives and mad scientists occupied the early pages of Superman comics much more often than superpowered villains and mutated freaks.

Despite Superman's extraterrestrial origins and unstoppable powers, he has remained an icon of the American way. Forward-looking comics like *The Dark Knight Returns* even made him a puppet of the U.S. government. Superman is the god made in America's image. And in embracing this American god, the popular American understanding of Jesus changed as well, a consequence of the fact that, as Bradford Wright observes, "each generation writes its own history, each reads its own comic books." Capon lays it out for us:

> The true paradigm of the ordinary American view of Jesus is Superman. . . . Jesus—gentle, meek and mild, but with secret, souped-up, more-than-human insides—bumbles around for thirty-three years, nearly gets himself done in for good by the Kryptonite Kross, but at the last minute, struggles into the phone booth of the Empty Tomb, changes into his Easter suit and, with a single bound, leaps back up to the planet Heaven.

In late 2004 rumors abounded that James Caviezel, fresh off his controversial role as Jesus in the film *The Passion of the Christ,* would play Superman in a forthcoming movie. Such cross-pollination, however speculative, is only the most recent, most explicit example of the blurred lines between what Capon calls "popular Christology" and Christologized popular culture. We are culturally conditioned to look for a hero—a messiah— and as such, casting Jesus as Superman seems the obvious choice.

But comic book readers who might also entertain the Christian faith can't marry Superman to Jesus, and so a question inevitably surfaces: who would win in a fight—Superman or Jesus?

We might try to dodge the question by suggesting that Superman wouldn't pick a fight and Jesus would turn the other cheek, but that would simply prompt a rephrasing of the question: who ought we to turn to in times of trouble? Who merits our affection and devotion?

THE COSMIC STRUGGLE

In fact, Superman might well have picked a fight with Jesus given the chance. Jesus made quick enemies of the champions of the status quo, and for all their flash, superheroes most often defend the status quo. In the name of free enterprise Superman would go after fascists and anarchists, and if his super-hearing were to have picked up on the chaos in the temple as Jesus attacked the moneychangers, he might have swooped in to save the day. In the name of the law Superman would go after lawbreakers, and if the religious authorities were to have made their case that Jesus was breaking the law by healing people on the sabbath, Superman might have taken Jesus out of the picture. And in the name of democracy, Superman might have bowed to the will of the crowd and sent Jesus to the cross.

But perhaps that's not being fair to Superman. After all, he is capable of independent thought and certainly intends to do right by the people he's sworn to protect. But Jesus might argue in return that lots of tragic evils start as good intentions. Inordinate love of country has led to the gross mistreatment of immigrants and dissidents, for example. Love of justice has blinded people of all ages to systemic flaws that often make lawbreaking seem to be a necessary evil—a lesson Green Arrow tried for years to teach Green Lantern. And love of truth has led to inquisitions and nuclear devastation. Good intentions suffer without the capacity to anticipate their consequences.

Yes, for all Superman's might, he doesn't make right. He doesn't make morality, he merely enforces the morality of the day and mirrors the aspirations to greatness and goodness reflected in his audience, as Mircea Eliade observes:

In the last analysis, the myth of Superman satisfies the secret long-ings of modern man who, though he knows that he is a fallen, lim-ited creature, dreams of one day proving himself an "exceptional person," a "Hero."

In this respect, Superman fulfills the obligation of his creation. He gives adolescents something to aspire to, some framework to make sense of the confusing world they find themselves in. Richard Reynolds prop-erly categorizes Superman as

an Oedipal myth for the century which invented the liminal states of teenager and adolescent, when physical mastery of the world precedes social mastery. Superman is adolescence writ large.

Jesus didn't create a new morality during his time on earth either. But unlike Superman, who serves the interests of his corporate creators by enforcing a mildly progressive status quo, Jesus used his time to refine morality as it was understood and to point people back to its originator. Evil is redefined as a consequence of humanity's fall from grace, pro-pelled by a fallen angel with a corrupted thirst for justice. But evil is not the final experience of humanity. In Jesus, God sets forth his agenda to deal ultimately with evil and to restore his creation to a state of grace, in a strategic move characterized by Nicholas Berdyaev:

Evil is a return to non-being, a rejection of the world, and at the same time it has a positive significance because it calls forth as a reaction against itself the supreme creative power of the good.

So whereas some superheroes, driven as they are by an "extra effort" that Richard Reynolds says "sums up the moral nature of the superhero," may ultimately grow weary and give up—as Martian Manhunter does in the epic *Crisis on Infinite Earths* ("I am tired of you humans! Tired of your evil! Tired of your lust for power!")—Jesus never gives up and never loses sight of the ultimate good that will come at the end of his story.

130

STRONG REACTIONS

One thing Jesus and Superman do have in common, however, is that they elicit strong reactions from people. Characters such as Batman and Green Arrow refer to Superman derisively as a "boy scout," suggesting that his view of the world is too idealized and sometimes affects his ability to see what the true crisis is. Other characters are in near-constant awe of him, and when trouble comes without Superman's intervention, they find their faith shaken.

Superman's writers divide along similar lines. For some, Superman can do no wrong, always arriving just in time to save the day. Others, such as the writers of the *Kingdom Come* storyline, explore what happens when Superman's intentions are misguided. As much good as Superman is able to do, his mistakes can have near-apocalyptic impact. Superman in the hands of his writers is essentially a tool, used for good or evil by whoever guides the pen.

Likewise, Jesus divides people into rigid categories. Those who declare their allegiance to him point to the power he displayed and the morality he championed, not to mention his heroic act of self-sacrifice at his crucifixion, which forgave us our debts and delivered us from evil. His resurrection cemented the deal for his followers: here is the unstoppable Son of God who does all things well and works all things to the good of those who love him.

Jesus certainly has his opponents, or at least his followers have opponents. Challengers to Jesus' legitimacy point to historic injustices done by the hands of Christians—the persecution of dissenters, the imperialistic results of missionary zeal, the stifling of creative thought, to name a few. Though few would presume to question Jesus' character, many cite the failings of his movement as reason enough not to sign up.

Others suggest that Jesus' power and influence have been overstated. They chalk up the recorded miraculous events of his life to embellished mythmaking by his followers, and they reject the evidence for his resurrection while pointing to other moral teachers as true sources for Jesus' thought.

I'm reminded of a comment by French political philosopher Voltaire: "If God did not exist, we would have created him." With the systematic erosion of trust that Jesus truly was God in the flesh, which grew out of modern rational thinking, and with the simultaneous changing of the guard in terms of what was considered politically and economically virtuous, Jesus seemed less and less like the hero our age needed. So in 1938 we created Superman to take his place.

CAN'T KEEP A GOOD MAN DOWN

Jesus isn't so easily snubbed, however. For all his merits, Superman is undeniably fictional, and Jesus remains undeniably real. Over time Superman predictably became less messianic and more iconic. The god of our making is first and foremost for our entertainment, and as such he is constrained by our imaginations. In *Origins of Marvel Comics*, Stan Lee's account of the Marvel Comics company history, he acknowledges our godlike sovereignty over the superheroes who model heroism for us, echoing language from the opening verses of the book of Genesis:

In the beginning Marvel created the Bullpen and the style.
And the Bullpen was without form, and was void;
and darkness was upon the face of the Artists.
And the Spirit of Marvel moved
upon the face of the Writers.

This attitude was made explicit in *Origins of Marvel Comics*, but it speaks to a temptation that plagues creative types, which Stan Lee evidenced long before the world took notice of him: during his senior year of high school, he climbed a ladder in his student newspaper office and wrote on the ceiling, "Stan Lee is God." Creations are subject to their creators no matter how much power they display.

Jesus, by contrast, continues to confound the imagination of historians, ethicists, religious and moral leaders, and laypeople of every stripe. Whereas everyone thinks they get the gist of what Superman is about, Jesus still sparks debate and hot tempers when his name comes up. The 2004 film *The Passion of the Christ*, for example, divided a moviegoing public into two vehemently opposed camps: thumbs way up versus thumbs way down. Many who accepted Jesus' claims of divinity and atonement for human sin loved the film, despite its graphic violence and artistic license, and made pilgrimage to see it even while, in some cases, marrying the content of the film to a conservative political agenda. On the other hand, many who had traditionally challenged the social agendas of these people decried the film as anti-Semitic and historically misleading. At the center stood Jesus, no less controversial than ever.

THE TROUBLE WITH ICONS

There is yet one common problem that both Superman and Jesus continue to suffer. Each has been surrounded by a culture that values him for his iconic status. The Superman logo is instantly recognizable, as is the central image related to Jesus: the cross.

In fact, it would hardly be shocking to see a kid in a mall somewhere wearing a blue shirt with a Superman logo, with a cross hanging around his neck. Both images send a cultural message: (1) I am powerful and good like Superman; (2) I am good and powerful like Jesus. Of course, nobody would hide behind this boy in a gunfight, even though Superman cannot be hurt by bullets. And nobody would bring a dead body to this boy assuming that he can bring someone back to life, even though Jesus is said to have done so on many occasions.

Jesus and Superman have become, for many, fashion statements, largely because they are no longer thought of as people so much as industries. In the case of Superman that's probably OK, since he is a modern invention of an American industry, designed to be put on and taken off. But to reduce Jesus thus is to strip him of his humanity, to separate him from the two thousand years' worth of cultural development and moral reflection and religious activism that has come out of his influence. It is to make light of his claims to humanity, not to mention his claims to divinity. It is to crucify Jesus all over again.

CONCLUSION

Becoming Super

*Batgirl lighted a candle in the **darkness.** She lighted a candle where there was no light.*

*There are a **few** people who care enough to help. There are only a small number. There are **fewer** who have the powers you have. But the **fewest** of all are those who care and have the powers.*

***I'd** like to make the world a better place. **I'd** better start now. **I'd** think all the people would like that. **I'd** is a short way of saying I would or I had or I should.*

*Hawkgirl wants to **serve** people. She wants to be of help to them. She has **served** people her whole life.*

THE SUPER DICTIONARY

Here's what comic book readers have come to know: Every day is an epic for a superhero, and so an epic is an everyday occurrence. Comic book readers have come to see cataclysm as commonplace, so much so that they are not put off by silly puns and one-liners in the heat of battle. In the experience of superheroes and the eyes of their fans, the world needs saving every day, so they might as well enjoy it. Matthew Pustz recognizes this development in the early Marvel approach to comic books:

> Many of its heroes . . . seemed to have great fun putting on costumes and fighting villains. At other times, Marvel heroes seemed to be radical individualists, dedicated to the benefits of macho vigor that come from standing up for oneself against apparently insurmountable odds.

People of Christian faith likewise recognize an ongoing crisis in their everyday experience: A fallen world shows daily symptoms of its fallenness even though the cure is in place. Christians are occasionally distracted by these symptoms, but deep down they know what the world needs and what their Lord wants them to do about it.

When comic book readers put down their books and re-enter the real world, they are reasonably confident that no superpowered criminal mastermind will take them hostage, that no alien force will threaten their city. So though they are attracted again and again to the epic antics of superheroes, their own everyday lives remain comparatively quiet.

"He has showed you . . . what is good. To act justly and to love mercy and to walk humbly with your God."

MICAH 6:8 NIV

When Christians put down their Scriptures, they have no such re-assurance that the threats they've read about—the passive distancing of a world from its loving Creator, the active plundering of that world by demonic forces—will not face them throughout the day. Yet though they are attracted again and again to the epic of faith in action found in the Bible, their own everyday lives often remain comparatively quiet.

What's appropriate for members of the comic book culture is fundamentally inappropriate for people of faith. And yet I've spent a whole book noting the overlapping influence of these two cultures on our definition of what is good. How do we properly put down the escapism of comic books without abandoning our sense of spiritual realities in our world?

ACT JUSTLY

"Justice!" It's what Daredevil demands as he faces his first enemy in the *Daredevil* film. It's one of Superman's big three ("truth, justice and the American way!"). It's also what fans expect from their heroes.

From the dawn of the comic book industry, justice has driven storytelling. *Superman* and *Batman* comics were early manifestations, but they were followed in rapid succession by other superheroes meting out justice to everyday fiends; by superhero collaborations such as the intentionally named Justice Society that faced major threats; by war comics in the 1940s and 1950s that asserted American righteousness; by 1950s horror and crime comics that displayed people getting their just deserts; and by new superheroes and teams throughout the turbulent 1960s, such as Green Arrow and Black Panther, whose more finessed understanding of justice saw systemic prejudice and economic stratification as wrongs needing to be righted.

The 1970s added political corruption and drug abuse to the list of injustices dealt with in comics. Spider-Man felt helpless as his best friend, Harry Osborne, fought an addiction. Captain America became the Nomad, giving up his name for a time in protest of the bad behavior of the Vietnam-era U.S. government. Friends and friendly governments had become victims and often the cause of injustice, so serving the cause of justice in the comic book world had, for a time at least, become a perplexing task.

American social realities of the 1980s helped to temporarily narrow comics' vision for justice. President Reagan took a no-nonsense hard line toward troublemakers—from Soviet dictators who led an "evil empire" to Middle Eastern upstarts and from labor organizers to environmental activists and artists. The nation took a sharp hawkish turn, celebrating film characters such as Rambo—an American war veteran out to get anyone who tainted his perception of American greatness— and Dirty Harry, a hard-nosed cop who fought punks wherever he found them.

In 1984 Bernard Goetz shot four young men who accosted him in a New York subway. In the process, he became for many a cultural icon— a symbol of the new law-and-order resistance. He was emulated in comics by characters such as the Punisher, whose sense of justice was not clouded by civil liberties or public safety, and Wolverine, whose obscure past left him with a barely controllable rage and a willingness to cross lines that superheroes never cross. Even Batman, as handled by writer Frank Miller, felt no constraint from the letter of the law.

"Marvel's central heroes may have been filled with angst and self-doubt, but they knew they had an obligation to fight evil and try to right the world's wrongs."

MATTHEW J. PUSTZ

The 1990s and beyond remained violent but recaptured the sense of ethical ambiguity from the 1970s. Gang violence became a public reality as celebrity hip-hop artists and actors were imprisoned or murdered. School shootings with social alienation as the apparent motivator sent shivers through the American suburbs. Domestic terrorism from groups who claimed religious or political righteousness, and televised court trials of the rich and famous in which legal wrangling won or lost cases, made justice a nebulous concept once again. Even the 2000 U.S. presidential election challenged the notion of straightforward right and wrong, as the simple task of counting votes degenerated into chaos.

Comics, therefore, have understandably had a difficult time pinning down justice. Christians are at an advantage here, because the Scriptures carry the influence of millennia and the authority of canonization. But practically speaking, dispensing justice remains a puzzle for Christians, in part because the Christian concept of justice must be tempered by a biblical call to love mercy.

LOVE MERCY

Mercy, at least popularly understood, is to justice what Superman is to Bizarro Superman. Everything normal to the one is completely alien to the other. As firm a grasp as justice has on Western culture, mercy has an unshakable appeal that, because it is so strange, we often don't know how to handle.

Mercy separates superheroes from vigilantes; mercy keeps superheroes from killing supervillains. In the film *Daredevil,* a hero willing to level a death sentence against an opponent has by the end changed his views with the simple realization "I'm not the bad guy." Bad guys kill; heroes practice mercy.

But nothing brings remorse like mercy. Merciful acts seem so noble and abnormal that any negative effects can trigger doubt and regret in the minds of the merciful—not to mention those who are indirectly affected by the act.

And yet there's something especially tragic when heroes choose not to practice mercy. Daredevil, holding the assassin Bullseye several stories off the ground, drops him so that he will never hurt anyone again. But in that moment, Daredevil forsakes mercy and to that degree forsakes heroism. We can point to that moment as early evidence of Daredevil's coming breakdown.

And when heroes practice mercy, even reluctantly, even in the face of ridicule, they ennoble themselves in our eyes. In *The Dark Knight Returns* an elderly Batman has the Joker trapped, after years of random sadistic violence that included the killing of Batman's partner Robin and (we learn elsewhere) the paralyzation of his colleague Batgirl. He is filled with a desperate rage that sees the Joker's death as the only solution to a world gone crazy. The Joker is at Batman's mercy, and Batman isn't feeling merciful.

Nevertheless, Batman can't bring himself to kill the Joker. The Joker, ridiculing and baiting Batman all along, exploits Batman's reluctant mercy by killing himself in such a way that Batman looks guilty. And yet, though the police and the government and the people of Gotham City see Batman from that point on as dangerous, we the readers know instinctively that he is good—that his act of mercy is proof of his nobility.

The best heroes daily wrestle to reconcile the commitment to justice that drives them to fight evil with the commitment to mercy that prompts them to protect life no matter what.

WALK HUMBLY WITH YOUR GOD

Where the Christian faith parts most starkly from the universe of superheroes is at the realization that we are not central characters in the story being recorded. Whereas comic book readers are encouraged to imagine themselves in the role of the title character, the biblical story is essentially one of a Creator, who is obviously a being separate from us, doing whatever it takes to restore his creation to himself.

"We were both ruthless and selfish, convinced of our inherent greatness and the worthlessness of all others."
SUNBURST, IN CRISIS ON INFINITE EARTHS

That being said, we are not filler in this story. God has drawn us not into the background but into the thick of it. We fall into four pivotal roles simultaneously: villain, victim, witness and partner.

We are *villains* in the sense that we have contributed directly to the crisis our Hero is confronting. It is our world that has marginalized, persecuted and exploited people; we the people have compromised the creation and discovered ways of doing evil. And you and I, in what we have done and what we have failed to do, have left our fingerprints all over the place.

But we are also *victims* in the sense that we have been victimized by the culture we've inherited and the moral failings of the people who surround us. We need deliverance, a restoration of order to the chaos we find ourselves in.

As such, we have the capacity to be *witnesses* to the way we are delivered. If we will only open our eyes, we will see the activity of our God. We will have plenty of stories to tell, stories that offer convincing evidence that the mysterious Hero of our everyday epic is not a menace to society but a Messiah par excellence.

"There are thousands of people out there—without powers like mine— . . . they're all ordinary people trying their best to keep this world from falling apart before its time."

SUPERGIRL, IN *CRISIS ON INFINITE EARTHS*

And beyond witnesses, we have the opportunity to be *partners*—like superhero Robin to Batman, like sidekick Jimmy Olsen to Superman, like middle-aged reporter Ben Urich to Daredevil—who find ourselves doing extraordinary things simply by imitating what we see our Hero doing.

Indeed Jesus is more than willing to share the thrill of his heroics with his followers; he goes so far as to promise them that they will do even greater things than they've seen him do.

But we must remember, these four roles are simultaneous. No matter how heroic we act alongside our Hero, we cannot deny our complicity in the wrongs we are addressing. No matter how strong we feel when empowered by our Creator, we cannot deny that we have been critically wounded by the battle.

So we are witnesses at all times to these ever-present, conflicting parts that we play, even as we give witness to the steady goodness of God, who does not change like our own shifting shadows (James 1:17). And this epic happens every day, which could bring us to despair if we let it, if we never looked beyond our sense of victimization or if we defined ourselves solely as villains. But when we open our eyes as witnesses to the heroism of God, we see the capacity for heroic action that he extends to us, and we realize that in spite of all we have suffered and all we have done, by the grace of God we could be heroes.

'Nuff said. Excelsior!

APPENDIX

How to Read a Comic Book

*Krypto can **read**. He can look at a book and understand the words. He has **read** all the books about Superboy.*

*Supergirl told her **story** to Superman. She told him what had happened to her. She always shares her **stories** with him.*

THE SUPER DICTIONARY

*T*he trouble with most superhero stories is that they're contained in comic books, and comic books are not an especially friendly medium to new readers. There's the stigma of immaturity that attends to them, such that to pick one up is to suggest to onlookers that you are too childish for "real" writing. Matthew Pustz characterizes the huddled masses of comic book readers as a prideful, persecuted minority: "The diverse communities of comic book readers are truly united by their devotion to the medium of comics itself, a medium mocked by some and ignored by others."

But even if you overcome the stigma, there's a tremendous variety of artistic style and storytelling that makes use of the medium: not every comic book has superheroes in it, and some have patently offensive material in them. And even if you find your way to the right comic book, you still have to find your way through it.

PICKING A COMIC

There are, essentially, three ways to pick a comic book: on a whim, on a recommendation or on purpose. In any case, you run the risk of being offended, confused or disappointed.

Comic book selection might seem to be a relatively private affair. You can, in fact, go a long way toward picking a book in private. Comic book producers are well-represented on the Internet, and at their sites you can survey character profiles, find out the current status of particular heroes and, in some cases, see samples of the characters in action, in the form of "dot-comics." Online booksellers sell graphic novels (an extensive but self-contained comic book) and in some cases provide editorial summaries and reader reviews. Fans maintain their own sites and can tell you what you want to know about a particular character, team, title, writer or artist.

"Our goal is that someday an intelligent adult would not be embarrassed to walk down the street with a comic magazine."

STAN LEE

That's all well and good, but to pick a comic thus is to prefilter a wide range of alternate selections. In contrast, some comic books can be found in libraries or in retail outlets ranging from grocery stores (where staff can offer little more than an aisle number in response to your questions) to shops devoted to comics and ancillary products. Here you can enter multiple universes and see the full cultural impact of the superhero genre. Between current issues and backlist titles, a comic book store offers near-total access to a character's history.

In addition, comic book stores bring you into direct contact with the genre's fiercely devoted fan base. Comic book shop regulars can offer overviews and synopses of many aspects of comic book history and culture. Storeowners can guide you to the type of art or storytelling you're looking for or help you find a good entry point into the medium. They will often also try to convert you to their way of life: late-night role-playing games, passionate discourse over the confusing details of current plots or heated debates over the limits of a particular hero's abilities. A trip into such a store can take much longer than you would expect, and on occasion it can overwhelm you to the point of despair.

In any event, whether in private or under the eager eyes of the comic fanboy, you'll eventually settle on a comic to read. Now all you have to do is figure out how to read it.

READING A COMIC

Comic books have something in common with child-safe lids on medicine bottles: the older you get, the less immediately obvious they become. Pustz highlights the challenge:

> Comic books demand a unique set of reading practices that many Americans lack. . . . Physically, the act of reading a comic book is unlike reading a traditional book. The eye cannot simply go from left to right in the same linear way it can when reading words only.

You might expect that, given the sheer number of pictures in a comic book and considering the likely vast experience you've had with newspaper comic strips, reading through a comic book will be easy—which will make your confusion as you read all the more frustrating.

Comic books are not generally organized in a way that is friendly to newcomers. Most issues begin by continuing a story that was left unconcluded in the issue previous. Issues are numbered sequentially, but series often relaunch to signify an editorial shift. Long-term characters have often had their origins retold to modernize their circumstances or provide a convenient starting point for new audiences. The industry in general presumes the reader's familiarity with the form, assuming that young readers, with more recent experiences of pictures and words working in tandem, will quickly assimilate. Nevertheless, with a little patience you can find your way through. Comic books are two art forms—sequential pictures and popular literature—working in concert. The words are a part of the pictures, and the pictures help to tell the story. The reader must be aware of both in order to fully appreciate the direction of the book.

PICTURES

The art of a comic book is generally active, with characters in the middle of some event—a fight, perhaps, or a flight from the moon to the earth. To prolong the sense of activity, art is set up in panels, with each panel representing one significant element of the overall story. A conversation or a battle may be spread out over many panels in order to give some sense of forward progression, but the amount of time represented in the space between panels (or "the gutter") is not consistent. As Scott McCloud notes in his *Understanding Comics,* "Space does for comics what time does for film." In some cases, a panel may even be a simultaneous view of a scene from another angle.

The reader is expected to assign meaning to what is not shown in the artwork, which makes even blank space important. McCloud, himself a comic book artist and writer, emphasizes this role: "Every act committed to paper by the comics artist is aided and abetted by . . . an equal partner . . . the reader." So, whereas critics might suggest that adding pictures to a story minimizes the role of the reader's imagination, the reader is actually never let totally off the hook. Reading a comic book requires your committed attention and your open imagination.

Still, following the story is a challenge, since text is broken into units not by paragraphs but by boxes, bubbles and balloons that can appear virtually anywhere in a panel to complement the artwork.

A George Perez-drawn *Fantastic Four* cover . . . was so densely packed with figures, there was no room to place text. Perez went to see Stan [Lee] and said, "Here's the cover. I'm stuck. I know it needs a blurb, but I can't figure out where to put it." Stan stared at the artwork briefly, and then pointed, "That man's raised arm. Bend it at the elbows." Immediately, the visual space opened up.

As such, the reader must submit to the guidance these text frames offer in order to follow the intended sequence.

WORDS

Much of what takes place in comic books is dialogue or monologue, indicated by bubbles and balloons. Thought is implied by using the more ethereal, cloudy bubbles; speech is conveyed in the solidly drawn balloons. Emphasis is suggested not only in how the letters are scripted but in how the text frames are drawn; a shouting match, for example, may be communicated by drawing jagged edges around the speech balloons.

Dialogue is read by moving among characters. Typically the sequence is suggested by the placement of speech balloons, so that by moving in general from left to right and from top to bottom, you get the story as it's meant to be gotten. Panic and confusion are suggested by clustering speech, so that balloons may overlap and be enhanced with thought bubbles; characters may even interrupt one another or be analyzing each others' comments in the midst of a conversation. The drama of a particular scene can be enhanced by breaking a character's speech into multiple balloons, implying dramatic pause or starting a new emphatic point.

Narrative rounds out the storytelling in comic books. It's usually placed in shaded boxes to indicate a strong break from the artwork. Narrative often gives the reader insights into a character's continuity—a sort of footnote to what's happening in the story's dialogue—but more often, it sets the scene or propels the plot. Occasionally, the boxed narration is "voiced" by a character rather than the writer, which allows for a completely different angle on the story to be shown in the art. You might be tempted to disregard the narrative boxes, but they are a key ingredient for the genre.

Sometimes the action being conveyed in the artwork requires that panels stray from the left-to-right, top-to-bottom format. You might read the wrong text frame by accident and find yourself confused. Stop and step back from the page to see what sent you in the wrong direction, or look for visual clues to establish that you in fact haven't missed any text. Many times text frames are sequenced using punctuation: three dots ending one frame link it to a nearby frame that begins with three dots. Double dashes are used in the same manner. Sometimes, in particularly complex sequences, the artist will include arrows to indicate the order of frames, but in most cases the artist's logic is there, waiting to be discovered. McCloud sees freedom from linear sequence as one of the great strengths of comics: "In comics, the past and future are real and visible and all around us."

Italic and bold type are ubiquitous in comic books, but they serve more a visual than a narrative function. If you've ever read the King James Version of the Bible and wondered why God wanted so much emphasis on the word *the* in a particular passage, you have some sense of the inadvertent confusion this convention can cause. In the case of the King James, italic type suggests simply that the text has been added or interpreted by the translator for clarity in the translation; in the case of comic books, bold and italic type simply add some color and weight to a text frame. No special emphasis should be given to such words.

Now, that should get you started. If this analysis is too confusing, or even if it is intriguing, you may want to read Scott McCloud's *Understanding Comics*, a full-length book in comic format that explains the mechanics very well. Otherwise, swallow your pride and get some help picking a comic book. And once you're done reading it, read it again. There's usually plenty going on to reward multiple readings.

ACKNOWLEDGMENTS

*I want to **thank** you for saving me, Superman. I want to say I am glad you did it. I have not **thanked** you enough.*

THE SUPER DICTIONARY

I've learned two things over the course of this book's publication: (1) everyone is one book away from being an irritating author; (2) having a book published is like having a year-long colonoscopy. The people listed below have been both patient as I learned the first lesson and anesthetic as I learned the second.

You have to be some kind of genetically enhanced idiot to make your "first" book about comic books; it greatly reduces the chances of your "second" book being taken seriously. Nevertheless, my peers and superiors at InterVarsity Press have been very supportive of my desire to write and, in particular, to write this book.

Al Hsu is my editor. Were our roles reversed, this book would have been written better and edited much less carefully. (That's why these acknowledgments are here at the back.)

Special thanks go out to Drew Blankman, who over time has stretched my thinking so much that it's lost its original shape; Gail Munroe and Maureen Tobey, who took great pains to indulge my juvenile desire for flip animation in the margin; Jim Erhart, a print buyer and a fan of superheroes from way back; Peter Mayer, a "marketing champion" who made a fool of me, and Karen Neidlinger, who pushed him around as he did it; Cindy Kiple, who dressed me up all pretty; Tony Parma, who makes for a super villain (good thing he's a good guy); Mark Eddy Smith, whose book *Tolkien's Ordinary Virtues* gave me the moxie to propose this book; and Joel Scandrett, Andy Shermer, Andrew Craft and Carey Aten, who keep me in touch with the comic book universe.

Elaina Whittenhall—the Sydney Bristow of copyeditors—whipped my book into shape, and Lisa Rieck—who has a proofreading eye like, I don't know, Hawkgirl—made sure I didn't end up looking like an idiot, which in the minds of many is a full-time job.

Come to think of it, IVP from front to back is full of good people and good friends. Here's to all of them. (Clink.)

Kristyn Komarnicki, the managing editor of *Prism* magazine, has given me opportunity after opportunity to practice at interviewing and writing and editing and missing deadlines. She also put me in touch with her brother, Todd Komarnicki, who along with my other interview subject, Frank E. Lee, made this project particularly enjoyable. Their experiences and insights were invaluable to the book.

Dave Micksch is a friend and a reliable critic, and if he were to have a superpower, it would involve cooking or painting or deciphering human nature. The Cotes gave me a great deal of support, not to mention adorable photographs of the kids in costume. Many others donated photographs as well, which ultimately had to be left out of the book. My thanks and regrets to you all.

My aunt Sarah funded my first blurring of the boundaries between Christianity and superheroes, for which I am grateful and apologetic. My parents gave me an allowance, took my picture on Santa Claus's lap while I was wearing my Halloween Robin costume, and encouraged me to read and write. They have no one to blame but themselves.

Acknowledgments

Kara Zimmerman, my wife and my friend, shares a name with the original Supergirl, which I find appropriate. She is not what you would call a fan of superheroes; nevertheless, she has been unflinchingly indulgent of my writing and a shameless promoter of the book. I owe her my thanks, several hours of our lives and a back rub.

NOTES

*"Supergirl likes to **study** her books. She likes to try to learn from the books. She has **studied** about history, animals, and how to catch Lex Luthor!"*

*"Atom is **writing** about being small. He is making words about being small on paper—a very small paper."*

THE SUPER DICTIONARY

Introduction

p. 11   "In . . . comic book-based stories" Brian Godawa, *Hollywood Worldviews* (Downers Grove, Ill.: InterVarsity Press, 2002), p. 28.

p. 13   "A DC comic" Bryon Stump, quoted in Matthew J. Pustz, *Comic Book Culture* (Jackson: University Press of Mississippi, 1999), p. 106. Stump actually prefers DC's more situational format; DC gradually embraced the more long-range storytelling pattern.

p. 13   "telling the company's readers" Ibid., p. 53.

p. 15   "The proliferation of comic books" (callout) Godawa, *Hollywood Worldviews*, p. 28.

p. 15   "*Super Dictionary*" Mary Z. Holmes, ed., *The Super Dictionary* (New York: Holt, Rinehart and Winston, 1978). All chapter epigraphs are taken from this resource.

pp. 17-18 "But as testing a car" I borrow this analogy from Mark Baker, *Religious No More* (Downers Grove, Ill.: InterVarsity Press, 1999).

Chapter One

p. 20   "The comic book . . . continues to be" Richard Reynolds, *Superheroes: A Modern Mythology* (Jackson: University Press of Mississippi, 1992), p. 7.

p. 20   "Comic book stories presented" (callout) Bradford W. Wright, *Comic Book Nation* (Baltimore: Johns Hopkins University Press, 2001), p. 160.

p. 22   "Superheroes are first and foremost" (callout) Scott McCloud, *Reinventing Comics* (New York: HarperCollins, 2000), p. 118.

p. 28   "The Hulk" (callout) Ang Lee, director of *The Hulk: The Motion Picture,* in *Entertainment Weekly,* June 6, 2003, p. 32.

Chapter Two

p. 32   "What makes Batman so different" (callout) Richard Reynolds, *Superheroes: A Modern Mythology* (Jackson: University Press of Mississippi, 1992), p. 67.

p. 33   "A compelling account" Frank Miller, *Batman: Year One* (New York: DC Comics, 1986).

p. 33   "[A superhero's] methods" (callout) Frank Vlamos, quoted in Bradford W. Wright, *Comic Book Nation* (Baltimore: Johns Hopkins University Press, 2001), p. 28.

p. 35   "Madness is" Alan Moore, Brian Bolland and John Higgins, *Batman: The Killing Joke* (New York: DC Comics, 1988), p.??.

p. 36   "The average man!" Ibid.

p. 38   "The negotiation of a character's heroism" (callout) Reynolds, *Superheroes: A Modern Mythology,* p. 41.

X-cursus

p. 42   "Imagine saving people" (callout) Dan Danko and Tom Mason, *Sidekicks* (New York: Little, Brown, 2003), p. 23.

p. 44   "Watch all" (callout) Ibid., p. 6.

Chapter Three

p. 47   "I am ready" The origin of the Batman, reprinted in Jules Feiffer, *The Great Comic Book Heroes* (New York: Bonanza, 1965), p. 70.

p. 48   "Why do you think" Frank Miller with Klaus Janson and Lynn Varley, *Batman: The Dark Knight Returns* (New York: DC Comics, 1986), p.??.

p. 49   "The authentic Iron Man" (callout) Richard Reynolds, *Superheroes: A Modern Mythology* (Jackson: University Press of Mississippi, 1992), p. 27.

p. 50   "Neither the police" Introduction to *Batman: A Death in the Family* (New York: DC Comics, 1988), postscript.

p. 51   "Tim temporarily surrendered" "The Wizard Preview: Robin," *Wizard* 150 (April 2004): 36.

p. 51   "Carrie Kelly" Miller, Janson and Varley, *Batman: The Dark Knight Returns.*

p. 51   "1-(900)" (callout) Ibid.

p. 53   "The self-reliant individualist" (callout) Reynolds, *Superheroes: A Modern Mythology,* p. 18.

p. 54   "In the comics miniseries" Joe Quesada, *Iron Man: Mask of the Iron Man* (New York: Marvel Comics, 1999).

p. 56   "Bruce—why are you" (callout) *Batman Returns* (Burbank, Calif.: Warner Brothers, 1992), videocassette.

p. 57   "We all tend" Jean Vanier, *Becoming Human* (New York: Paulist, 1998), p. 158.

Chapter Four

p. 60   "From a psychological angle" (callout) William Moulton Marston, quoted in Maria Reidelbach, *Completely Mad* (Boston: Little, Brown, 1991).

p. 63   "Continuity adds depth" Matthew J. Pustz, *Comic Book Culture* (Jackson: University Press of Mississippi, 1999), p. 129.

p. 63   "The more comics published" (callout) Richard Reynolds, *Superheroes: A Modern Mythology* (Jackson: University Press of Mississippi, 1992), p. 38.

p. 64   "The Batman we meet" Frank Miller with Klaus Janson and Lynn Varley, *Batman: The Dark Knight Returns* (New York: DC Comics, 1986).

p. 65   "Matt Murdock loved Elektra" Frank Miller with Klaus Janson, *The Elektra Saga* (New York: Marvel Entertainment Group, 1989).

p. 66   "In a poignant moment" Ibid., p. 152.

p. 67   "His finest hour" Frank Miller and David Mazzucchelli, *Daredevil: Born Again* (New York: Marvel Entertainment Group, 1987).

Chapter Five

p. 70   "The primary function served by women" Bradford W. Wright, *Comic Book Nation* (Baltimore: Johns Hopkins University Press, 2001), pp. 184-85.

p. 70   "In the world of comics" (callout) Andrew D. Arnold, "Drawing In the Gals," *Time,* February 16, 2004, p. 97.

p. 72   "The (male) reader" (callout) Richard Reynolds, *Superheroes: A Modern Mythology* (Jackson: University Press of Mississippi, 1992), p. 37.

p. 73   "a fourteen-year-old" Scott McCloud, *Reinventing Comics* (New York: HarperCollins, 2000), p. 100.

p. 75   "Perception affects" (callout) Ibid., p. 82.

p. 75   "Why not complete" Mark Gruenwald and Ralph Macchio, *Marvel Two-in-One* 55 (September 1979): 6.

p. 76   "Open-minded white writers" (callout) Wright, *Comic Book Nation,* p. 249.

p. 79   "Thomas Merton recognized" Merton, quoted in Brian J. Mahan, *Forgetting Ourselves on Purpose* (San Francisco: Jossey Bass, 2002), p. 171.

p. 79   "Frederick Buechner reveals" Buechner, quoted in ibid., p. 122.

X-cursus

p. 83   "It's considered normal" (callout) Scott McCloud, *Understanding Comics* (Northampton, Mass.: Kitchen Sink Press, 1993), p. 139.

p. 84   "I used to wait" (callout) Hobart Lindsey, quoted in Matthew J. Pustz, *Comic Book Culture* (Jackson: University Press of Mississippi, 1999), p. 208.

Chapter Six

p. 87   "Comic books were really" (callout) Bradford W. Wright, *Comic Book Nation* (Baltimore: Johns Hopkins University Press, 2001), p. 89.

p. 88   "The comic book market" Ibid., p. 134.

p. 90   "Confronted with the sober realization" Ibid., p. 227.

p. 92   "the world's first creedal nation" Richard John Neuhaus, *Doing Well and Doing Good* (New York: Bantam, 1992), n.p.

Chapter Seven

p. 97   "The Avengers are there" (callout) Geoff Johns, Scott Kolins and Steve Sadowski, *The Avengers: The Search for She-Hulk* (New York: Marvel Entertainment Group, 2004).

pp. 98-99   "the original JLA" Kurt Busiek, introduction to Mark Waid, Brian Augustyn and Barry Kitson, *JLA: Year One* (New York: DC Comics, 1999).

p. 99	"rational, mature" Ibid.
p. 100	"There's a long history" *JLA/Avengers* 1-4 (New York: DC Comics/Marvel Entertainment Group, 2003-2004).
p. 102	"In American society" Bradford W. Wright, *Comic Book Nation* (Baltimore: Johns Hopkins University Press, 2001), p. 13.
p. 102	"As the culture of subsequent decades" Ibid., p. 229.
p. 103	"Once the odds" Jules Feiffer, quoted in ibid., p. 13.

Chapter Eight

p. 105	"The words of creeds" Dorothy L. Sayers, *The Mind of the Maker* (San Francisco: HarperSanFrancisco, 1987), p. 26.
p. 106	"In the Marvel Comics universe" Matthew J. Pustz, *Comic Book Culture* (Jackson: University Press of Mississippi, 1999), p. 49.
p. 107	"a crude, exaggerated" Bradford W. Wright, *Comic Book Nation* (Baltimore: Johns Hopkins University Press, 2001), p. xiv.
p. 107	"Thor enjoys" Richard Reynolds, *Superheroes: A Modern Mythology* (Jackson: University Press of Mississippi, 1992), pp. 58, 60.
p. 108	"when asked to pray" John Teter, *Get the Word Out* (Downers Grove, Ill.: InterVarsity Press, 2003), p. 104.
p. 108	"As Marvel insisted" Wright, *Comic Book Nation*, p. 244.
p. 110	"In a medium associated with escapism" (callout) Scott McCloud, *Reinventing Comics* (New York: HarperCollins, 2000), p. 35.
p. 110	"Heroes need to triumph" Reynolds, *Superheroes: A Modern Mythology*, p. 82.
pp. 111-112	"Power shall be mine!" Dr. Vreekill, "Batman and Robin visit the 1940 New York World's Fair," quoted in ibid., p. 23.

Chapter Nine

p. 114	"Author Walt Wangerin" Walter Wangerin Jr., *Reliving the Passion: Audio Pages* (Grand Rapids, Mich.: Zondervan, 1992).
p. 115	"Have you ever" (callout) Neil Zawacki, *How to Be a Villain* (San Francisco: Chronicle, 2003), p. 140.
p. 116	"The solution" Dan Jurgens, Ron Frenz and Joe Rubinstein, *Superman* 123 (May 1997): 8.
p. 116	"The 1989" James D. Hudnall and Eduardo Barreto with Adam Kubert, *Lex Luthor: The Unauthorized Biography* (New York: DC Comics, 1989).
p. 117	"One thing" (callout) Dan Danko and Tom Mason, *Sidekicks* (New York: Little, Brown, 2003), p. 68.
p. 119	"John Byrne" John Byrne, *Fantastic Four: The Trial of Galactus* (New York: Marvel Entertainment Group, 1989).
p. 120	"A herald precedes" Kurt Busiek and Alex Ross, *Marvels*, book 3, *Judgment Day* (New York: Marvel Comics, 1994).
p. 120	"I am power" Byrne, *Fantastic Four: The Trial of Galactus*.
p. 122	"Follow that logic" Henri Blocher, *Evil and the Cross*, trans. David G. Preston (Downers Grove, Ill.: InterVarsity Press, 1994), p. 26.
p. 122	"evil becomes" Ibid., p. 24.
p. 123	"For a humanity" Ibid., p. 13.

Chapter Ten

p. 126   "Faster than a speeding bullet" Robert Farrar Capon, *Hunting the Divine Fox* (New York: Seabury Press, 1974), p. 90.

p. 127   "Twentieth-century America demanded" (callout) Bradford W. Wright, *Comic Book Nation* (Baltimore: Johns Hopkins University Press, 2001), p. 10.

p. 128   "each generation" Ibid., p. xiii.

p. 128   "The true paradigm" Capon, *Hunting the Divine Fox,* p. 90.

p. 129   "In the last analysis" Mircea Eliade, *Myth and Reality,* trans. Willard R. Trask (New York: Harper & Row, 1963), p. 185, quoted in Brian Godawa, *Hollywood Worldviews* (Downers Grove, Ill.: InterVarsity Press, 2002), p. 29.

p. 130   "an Oedipal myth" Richard Reynolds, *Superheroes: A Modern Mythology* (Jackson: University Press of Mississippi, 1992), p. 66.

p. 130   "Evil is a return to non-being" Nicholas Berdyaev, *The Destiny of Man,* translated by Natalie Duddington, quoted in Dorothy L. Sayers, *The Mind of the Maker* (San Francisco: HarperSanFrancisco, 1987), p. 99.

p. 130   "sums up" Reynolds, *Superheroes: A Modern Mythology,* p. 41.

p. 132   "In the beginning" Stan Lee, *Origins of Marvel Comics* (New York: Simon & Schuster, 1974), quoted in Matthew J. Pustz, *Comic Book Culture* (Jackson: University Press of Mississippi, 1999), p. 49.

p. 132   "Stan Lee is God" Jordan Raphael and Tom Spurgeon, *Stan Lee and the Rise and Fall of the American Comic Book* (Chicago: Chicago Review, 2003).

Conclusion

p. 136   "Many of its heroes" Matthew J. Pustz, *Comic Book Culture* (Jackson: University Press of Mississippi, 1999), p. 50.

p. 138   "In 1984 Bernard Goetz" John Shelton Lawrence and Robert Jewett, *The Myth of the American Superhero* (Grand Rapids, Mich.: Eerdmans, 2002), pp. 118-20.

p. 138   "Marvel's central heroes" (callout) Pustz, *Comic Book Culture,* p. 49.

p. 139   "And when heroes practice mercy" Frank Miller with Klaus Janson and Lynn Varley, *Batman: The Dark Knight Returns* (New York: DC Comics, 1986).

p. 140   "We were both ruthless and selfish" (callout) Marv Wolfman and George Pérez, *Crisis on Infinite Earths* (New York: DC Comics, 2000), p. 330.

p. 141   "There are thousands" (callout) Supergirl, quoted in ibid.

Appendix

p. 143   "The diverse communities" Matthew J. Pustz, *Comic Book Culture* (Jackson: University Press of Mississippi, 1999), p. 68.

p. 144   "Our goal is" (callout) Stan Lee, quoted in Jordan Raphael and Tom Spurgeon, *Stan Lee and the Rise and Fall of the American Comic Book* (Chicago: Chicago Review, 2003), p. 125.

p. 145   "Comic books demand" Pustz, *Comic Book Culture,* p. 122.

p. 145   "Space does for comics" Scott McCloud, *Understanding Comics* (Northampton, Mass.: Kitchen Sink Press, 1993), p. 7.

p. 146   "Every act" Ibid., p. 68.

p. 147   "A George Perez-drawn" Raphael and Spurgeon, *Stan Lee,* p. 151.

p. 148   "In comics, the past" McCloud, *Understanding Comics,* p. 104.

David A. Zimmerman (left, with sister Elaine and brother Steve) is an associate editor for InterVarsity Press. A lifelong comic book fanboy, he has written on issues related to superheroes for *Student Leadership Journal* and BustedHalo.com. He is a regular contributor to *Prism* magazine and has written on a wide range of subjects in various print and online publications.

In his weekly blog, "Strangely Dim," Zimmerman picks apart the routines of his life and finds what's wonderfully absurd and absurdly wonderful about being human day by day. Along the way he raises questions that only God could answer and waits expectantly with the rest of us for God to post a comment.

Zimmerman and his wife live in Lombard, Illinois.

Access *Strangely Dim* at

www.ivpress.com/campus/sd/

A discussion guide related to this book is available online from the IVP book page
www.gospelcom.net/cgi-ivpress/book.pl/code=3260

and the InterVarsity Christian Fellowship website:
www.intervarsity.org/biblestu/gigs/

Index of Characters